BOUND FOR SHADY GROVE

Bound for Shady Grove

Steven Harvey

To David —
a fellow banjoist —
thanks for coming tonight
and sharing in the
music.
Best wishes,
Steve Harvey

UNIVERSITY OF GEORGIA PRESS ATHENS AND LONDON

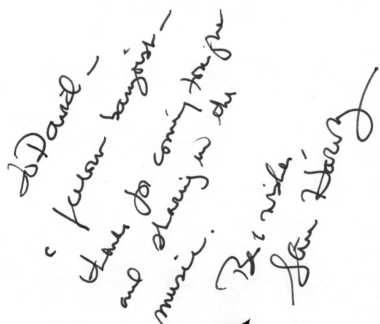

Published by the University of Georgia Press
Athens, Georgia 30602

Designed by Erin Kirk New
Set in 10 on 15 Galliard by G & S Typesetters
Printed and bound by Maple-Vail Book Manufacturing Group

The paper in this book meets the guidelines for permanence and durability of the Committee on Production Guidelines for Book Longevity of the Council on Library Resources.

Printed in the United States of America

04 03 02 01 00 C 5 4 3 2 1

Library of Congress Cataloging-in-Publication Data
Harvey, Steven, 1949 June 9–
Bound for Shady Grove / Steven Harvey.
p. cm.
ISBN 0-8203-2197-4 (alk. paper)
1. Folk music—Appalachian Region—History and criticism. 2. Harvey, Steven, 1949 June 9– 3. Authors—United States—Biography. I. Title.
ML3551.7.A57 H37 2000
781.62′130758—dc21 99-047566

British Library Cataloging-in-Publication Data available

For my daughters, Nessa and Alice

Though the sound overpowers,
Sing again, with your dear voice revealing
A tone
Of some world far from ours,
Where music and moonlight and feeling
Are one.

—*Shelley*

Peaches in the summertime,
Apples in the fall,
If I can't have little Shady Grove,
Don't want anyone at all.

—*Traditional mountain song*

Little birdie, little birdie
Come sing to me your song
I've a short time to be here,
And a long time to be gone.

—*Traditional mountain song*

CONTENTS

ACKNOWLEDGMENTS

I want to thank all of the people who ever sang or played music with me, especially the members, past and present, of Butternut Creek and Friends: Don, Jennifer, Rachel, Mindy, Butch, Bill, and Sue. When we're apart, there's sorrow in the wind.

The author and publisher gratefully acknowledge the following publications in which essays in this volume first appeared: *The Oxford American,* "Mountain Minor"; *Five Points,* "The Devil by Surprise" and "Bluing"; *Brightleaf,* "Soldier's Joy" and "The Lydian Mode"; *Atlanta Magazine,* "November Fields"; *Journal of Kentucky Studies,* "The Oldest Answer," *Appalachian Heritage,* "Dulcet Melodies"; *The Florida Review,* "High Lonesome"; *The Seneca Review,* "The Drone"; *The Fourth Genre,* "Big Scioty."

PREFACE

I type the name "Hedy West" and watch the title "Five Hundred Miles" float in blue capitals onto the computer screen, and for a time I sit back in my chair and just look at the words. It's true, I think. Here in my office at a small college in a remote section of the Appalachian Mountains, I am about five hundred miles from Kansas, where I was born, and Illinois, where I grew up, not to mention New Jersey, where I learned to play the guitar and first heard that song. I am a good five hundred miles from anywhere I could call home.

I double-click on the title—wait a moment while my machine appears to drift through the blue-clouded world of cyberelectronics—and the song, printed in blue appears: "FIVE HUNDRED MILES, Hedy West, copyright Atzal Music, Inc." The cursor blinks, awaiting my next command. Hedy West was raised in Carrollton, Georgia, just around the mountain from where I live now. She grew up just down the road, I realize, and yet she put that song on my lips years ago when I was a boy living on the outskirts of Trenton, and suddenly, without the help of the computer, I'm transported to a basement den in New Jersey more than thirty years ago, where a teenager sits Indian style in front of a stereo, strumming simple chords and singing about being a long, long way from home.

I never think of New Jersey as home, or even a part of my life anymore. Except for rest stops on the turnpike, I have not visited there in years, and my accent, I know, has been softened by nearly three decades of living in the South, my adopted home. But in one sense New Jersey *is* home, because it was there that I learned to play the guitar, trying out my adolescent voice, which was settling into a raspy tenor, and wrapping my fingers around songs that had their start in the mountains where I live now. In a suburb of Trenton, with Route 1 just down the road and Princeton a bicycle ride away, I learned "Tom Dooley," my first folk song, and "Mary Hamilton," and, of course, "Five Hundred Miles," a title that, if nothing else, marked off the distance those songs had to travel to find their way to me.

The house was split level, suburban, and the stereo was a console in a blond Danish modern cabinet with a tall, curved changer for dropping a stack of albums one at a time and a heavy green tone arm that looked like army issue. My spot was on the floor right in front of one of the speakers, staring at an album cover with a guitar in my lap. In my memory, three faces—Peter, Paul, and Mary—stare back. I wish the source of this primordial moment in my life could be classier: a Dock Boggs album, say, or even one by Hedy West herself. There is something *obvious* about a folk music *frisson* that finds its beginnings in Peter, Paul, and Mary, but there you have it. In matters of love, we have no choice.

Who knows what I was like, then, listening to songs about flowers and cruel wars escaped and biblical stories and nursery rhymes? Innocent, I guess. The nursery rhymes, in particular, are cloying now, I realized after I turned off the computer at my office, went home, and to the amusement of my wife put on the old scratchy album and listened. She listened, too, and we both winced a few times. Mary Travers singing "Anyone round my base is *it*" simply does not work. Did it ever? But hearing the album afresh after all those years, I was struck by how lush and gorgeous the music is, rich, sweet guitars and vocals, especially the men's voices, and I know, all over again, why Mary Travers cried the first time she heard Paul Stookey sing.

The cover, as much as the music, held me as a boy, and looking at it now between fingers much older, I think I can see why. Peter and Paul in dark jackets and ties sporting identical goatees and Mary, trim, young, and smiling, sitting on a stool between them, her famous blond hair glowing, not as straight or long as it later became, but shoulder length with a little flip curl. The three of them are on the stage of the Bitter End coffeehouse in Greenwich Village with the letters PP&M enclosed in a yellow pastel heart chalked on the brick wall behind them. I was in love.

"Just look at their faces, listen to their songs," the liner notes recommended, and I did, for hours on end, tracing the chalked lines with my finger while hearing "Constant Sorrow" or "Bamboo" or "Lemon Tree." Over the years I've memorized every scratch on this much-played disc so that the blips have become part of the songs for me, but somehow, despite scratches and time, it remains nearly flawless now as it did then.

Where have all the flowers gone?

Five hundred miles, I suppose, away from a boy in front of the stereo playing the guitar.

Hedy West learned music from her family in Carrollton. Her uncle Gus and her father, the poet Don West, taught her the old songs, and her grandmother showed her how to play the traditional banjo. She learned the mountain way by watching and doing. Her banjo playing, especially on the old ballads like "The Wife of Usher's Well" and "Little Matty Groves," is haunting, and her singing voice a cold wind, it seems, riding along any melody she plucks.

After a successful performance in Boone, North Carolina, in 1956, when she was seventeen, she began touring coffeehouses in New York, no doubt hanging around with the likes of Peter Yarrow, Paul Stookey, and Mary Travers, who were there then as well. In 1961—just about the time that my family moved to New Jersey—she wrote "Five Hundred Miles." She drew on an old ballad, "The Railroader's Lament," but, in the way of folk singers, she made it her own. Two years later, when I had my first guitar lesson, Peter, Paul, and Mary cut the track for their premier album.

Seeing Hedy West's name on the computer screen, I followed the songs back, the melody leading inexorably, like a slow, meandering creek, to that boy I once was in New Jersey, and I realized that music has, indeed, taken me on a long journey, a journey that became this book. The first Saturday of every month in those days I grabbed up my allowance money and rode a bicycle from our house in Lawrence Township to the bookstore at Princeton University with one purpose: to buy a new album. The trip was long—more than a half hour of steady pedaling along a highway that wound through wooded countryside—so I made a morning of it, packing a lunch. There was one town along the way, Lawrenceville, with a prep school behind a long stone wall, but beyond that nothing but trees and fields. Trees covered the road like a canopy in spots, and light fell in patches here and there, dashing across my sleeves and shirtfront and face as I coasted along. When I came to the final stretch—the curve in the road that led to the university—I pumped hard, parking my bike in front of the U-Store.

I usually spent an excruciating hour in front of the record rack deciding whether to leave Joan Baez or Bob Dylan or the Kingston Trio behind—the decision was a weighty one. Once made, I paid for my prize, propped it in the metal basket on the bike, and headed back down the road, with the hope of new music ahead as I closed the gap between me and home.

When I moved to the mountains of Georgia years later to take a job as an English teacher at a small college, I believed I had outgrown the guitar and folk music. It had been a long time since I had ridden a bike to get an album. Teaching consumed me and confirmed my love for literature, and this new mistress, a plain lover who came in soft and hard covers, with a pretty face that perpetually wore a troubled look, was jealous indeed. Silence, a sanctuary marked off in unuttered meters, became my companion, and the words I found at the edge of silence wore the austere garb of mere speech, my music reduced to a hum or whistle as I walked down Appleby Drive to the classroom. Meanwhile my guitar waited like a patient, aging paramour. Strings rusted, struts snapped loose, and the neck warped a little, so that I could not play songs with ease, even if I had wanted to.

Always the old songs were in my head, but this body of memorized literature was unrefreshed by any newly learned tunes, so the songs turned into artifacts, like souvenir photos of a trip you'll never take again. My "repertoire," such as it ever was, dwindled down to a few numbers. "Five Hundred Miles" was one, but every time I sang it I felt as if I *had* missed the train, and sometimes when I picked the instrument up, strumming rusty strings, I felt as if I were five hundred miles from whatever it had meant to me. Some strut of the soul had come unglued.

After fifteen years of teaching, with the music in me drying up, I was saved, appropriately enough, in church, a small Episcopal congregation in a rented wooden building at the end of a country road. I remember nothing about the sermon or the service itself. I remember trees in the window, springtime dogwoods that we are famous for in the mountains, the petals of one shoved up into the windowpane, and other trees dotting the newly green hillside. I remember the folk choir, shaggy-haired minstrels in their Sunday best, a thicket of guitar necks, music stands, and congas, giving newly minted Christian hymns a familiar sound. "Lord, Take My Yes," they sang, the sentimental words riding strummed chords out of windows and into the woods, each "yes" a spot of white in a dark world.

The next day I fetched the guitar out of the closet and bought new strings.

Although the guitar has an important place in mountain music now, it was a late addition and not a natural fit with the old sounds of ballads and fiddle tunes sung here since whites first settled the region. Arriving in the mail in inexpensive Sears and Roebuck models in the twenties, the guitar smoothed off the rough edges of mountain tunes. The fretted keyboard, rich in chromatic possibilities, offered a break with the pentatonic and modal sound, allowed for accidentals, and encouraged harmony and blend rather than a plunky banjo counterpoint. Many of the modal songs simply dropped out of the repertoire or were changed, losing their haunting melodies in favor of the prettier harmonies that the chords of the guitar offered. By stripping away the oddity of the old songs, the guitar became the bridge between the unique music of the mountains and the music of popular culture.

It was a bridge that I eventually crossed, going the other way, by putting a banjo on my knee and a dulcimer in my lap. But it was the guitar that started it all for me. It surrounded me with sounds, the strange but hauntingly familiar songs that are my birthright, telling me who I am. My ancestors had been among those who traveled from Ireland and England to the New World bringing their songs, and occasionally a fiddle, with them as they headed west. My grandmother, I know, played a mandolin, beautifully, my father told me, and beautiful or not, it must have been inspiring because my father regretted all his life that he did not play a musical instrument, an error he corrected with me. He never encouraged me in sports or hunting—activities he did superbly. The only way Dad ever lived vicariously through me was in my music, which he loved too, and I could always get him to bang out a rhythm on his knee with his hands, his best instrument. My playing took him back, I think, at least five hundred miles from what he had become, to something he had lost.

But a bridge goes both ways, and the guitar, unexpectedly, took me to the opening pages of the poetry anthology for my classes as well, pages I used to skip. I taught the anonymous song lyrics of the thirteenth and fourteenth centuries as well as the ancient popular ballads and began to see literature in new ways. I played ballads for the students, songs like "Rollin', Rollin'," a southern version of the Child ballad "The Twa Sisters," and I studied the influence of ballads collected by Thomas Percy and Francis Child on writers like Wordsworth. I learned that one of Shelley's many loves was Jane Williams, who played the guitar for him. The poem he wrote for her mentions the "tinkling" sound of the instrument and, in lines which, for me, are the ambition of all poetry and music, imagines a world "far from ours" where "music and moonlight and feeling are one."

When I joined the folk choir, I rediscovered, to my joy, that the fingers never forget. It was not just songs that came back to me as the calluses at my fingertips toughened, or tunes or chord patterns, but the part of me that knew and loved the songs came back in veils of my former pleasure. An old lover had returned to my life, and she was, despite dings and nicks, as lovely as she had been on those nights years before when she first took in a lonely boy. Soon I was playing in groups, singing in coffeehouses, and going to weekend gatherings. Inevitably,

I suppose, I started writing about the music in my area and the people who make it.

I recently put in an evening at the home of Chuck and Peggy Patrick, who live in a house in one of the coves near Brasstown, North Carolina, just across the border from me. Chuck is a blacksmith: his forge and work shed are near the house. The house itself is a large but cozy cabin where he and Peggy raise a family of happy, home-schooled children and make great music. Chuck and Peggy are members of the old-time music group Ross Brown and Friends, and Ross, the well-known left-handed fiddler, was there along with Rachel Caviness, their bass player.

They are all better musicians than I am, especially Ross. He is in his eighties and has played throughout the mountains of Georgia and North Carolina since he was a boy. He has gone on musical tours of Europe and recently did a performance at the Olympics in Atlanta. Most of the time I kept my banjo in the case, but since Don Fox, the guitarist for the group, was not there, I played along on guitar in the background. Afterward Ross told my friend Rachel that there was nothing wrong with my playing, I just needed more practice, a fact I brought home with vindicated pride to a family that endures the racket I make during every free moment of the day.

The Patrick house is a wonderful place to sing mountain songs. The walls are exposed wood, decorated with instruments including a grand-looking old five-string that no longer stays in tune and a great viola that Chuck played in school. Off to the side, directly behind the chair where Ross sat, is a wood stove that Jacob, Chuck's son, kept loaded. Mary Anne, the Patricks' daughter, was out in the kitchen baking a cake, so between songs Peggy had to shout instructions about how much butter to use and where to find the eggbeater. We sat in wooden chairs in a circle, Ross leading off each tune, while the rest of us, his friends, tried to keep up. After each song the kids gave us a round of applause from other rooms in a place where moonlight and music and feeling are, in fact, one.

When I watch the fingers of Peggy's left hand fly over the banjo strings and her other hand flip-flop with an effortless drop thumb in happy syncopation, I know that, after more than twenty years of living in the mountains, I am just at the tip, at the beginning of finding my way back into the music of my adopted place and will, I suppose, never feel entirely at home in the mountains. People in Appalachia are friendly but slow to take in strangers, especially from the North. My family never went through the cultural isolation that is the defining characteristic of mountain life—a fact symbolized by the way the mountains hem people in on all sides—and I myself am slow to warm up to the idea that my home is Georgia. The mountains are not, as one of our famous residents has put it, within me, and I have mentally lived out of a suitcase since I arrived.

If there is a way that the mountains seem like home, one clue that this is where I belong, it is not my felt hat or my porch overlooking a hillside of service and dogwood or the quarter of a century I have spent teaching in the hills, but the image of that boy in front of a record player in Lawrence Township, New Jersey, a guitar in his lap, singing songs that began five hundred miles away in the mountains where I now live.

The essays in this book chronicle the trip. *Bound for Shady Grove* is not a history of the mountains or mountain music or mountain life, and I am certainly not an expert in any of these areas, though I have drawn on the work of scholars, folklorists, and musicologists to tell my tale. Nor is this book a memoir of a mountain man, since I can't handle a chain saw, a rifle, a campfire, or a pint of moonshine without endangering the lives of all around me. In the course of writing the book, it is true, I have not gotten any worse at the guitar and learned how to plunk out a few tunes on the banjo, but I am not a serious musician, and, in the end, this is not a book about music. I am, instead, a dedicated amateur—a mere lover of mountain song—and this book of personal essays is about where music can take the likes of me, where, in fact, music can take any of us. The way I recognize myself in north Georgia is in the simple fact that I have sung these songs with love most of my life, no matter where I have lived. In these essays I follow a thread in the songs of my adopted home until they take me to a place I know, and have known, all of my life.

But there is more to it than that. All songs, I have found in writing this book, are lullabies, transforming the landscape of our orphaned lives, whether we are in a city, the country, or a desert, into a home. That is the thousand-mile round trip that we all can make. When Peggy sings "Barbara Allen" while Chuck plays the mandolin and her daughter bakes a cake in the kitchen nearby, I see—in some dark recesses of the imagination—the pioneer grandmother I never met put the instrument in her lap and hear her sing our story. As I join in, I feel in the guitar a deep resonance. This book is about music as a home, whether we are away from home or not, and the story of my coming home in unfamiliar country is the story of anyone's homecoming. I know I'm not there, of course. Located on the cross tie of some train track in the middle of the cyberspace of contemporary American life, I am forever bound for Shady Grove and may never arrive, but the dulcimer in my lap and tune on my lips tells me I'm headed in the right direction. Perhaps if I put in another five hundred miles or so, I'll find my way back to where I belong after all.

The Ionian Mode

According to Dad Ritchie, you tune her like this: bim, bim, bam; two strings alike and the bass string five tones lower. The singing school master sings it "so," "so," "do." . . . And according to the Greeks, this is called the Ionian mode.

—Jean Ritchie, *The Appalachian Dulcimer*

We begin in the Ionian mode, the mode of spring. Bits of winter cling to it in the drone, which, played alone, has the groan of an old man rising from his chair, uncertain where he is, death hovering in corners, but the scale itself, played against this monotone, is all lightness, rising effortlessly, it seems, like a winged seed, floating past the gray trunks of trees to open ground, where it whirls reluctantly to moist earth.

On the lap dulcimer, an instrument that mountain people inherited and, like the banjo and fiddle and bones, made their own, the melodies come in ancient diatonic scales, the seven modes: Ionian, Mixolydian, Dorian, Aeolian, Phrygian,

Lydian, and Locrian. Each mode, emerging by different tunings out of its drone strings, has its own feel, its own season. Taken together they tell our story, a love story of new life emerging happily, struggling into adulthood and the possibility of love, flirting with cynicism, maturing into woe, and ultimately giving in to forces larger than human love can redeem, returning, inevitably, to the drone from which it was created.

The best way to picture these modulations—and to see the relationships among the modes—is with the modestar, created by Bertrand Bronson, the folklorist and musicologist who arranged the modes along the points of a seven-sided star. Using his diagram, I can move my finger, clockwise, from one point of the star to the next through the various modes, and trace the evolution from the brassy, happy Ionian mode of spring to the eerie, obsessive, and otherworldly Locrian mode, the winter mode in our future, touching in order all the modes between. As one scale gives way to the next, shedding certain intervals and picking up new ones, we progress through a series of emotions as well, the star representing the range of our feelings, the modes telling the story of a life as the story of the year.

The Ionian is the most common mode for the dulcimer. Bim, bim, bam, *Jean Ritchie's father liked to say when tuning to that mode.* Sol, sol, do. *And "Go Tell Aunt Rhody," the first song most people learn on the dulcimer, is a gradual movement up and down the Ionian scale. In the song new life emerges from death. The old gray goose that Aunt Rhody saved for a featherbed has died—it happened on a Friday night behind the woodshed. The tune itself—we all know it—is stately and slow. And yet, there is a lilt there, the hint of fresh possibilities. The goose left a gaggle of nine little goslings, and though they must fend for themselves alone, their number—the fecundity built into life—offers hope. Who, after all, accepts the command to "go tell Aunt Rhody"? Who brings news of death to the old?*

The children, of course.

So we begin, in the Ionian mode, the mode of spring.

Mountain Minor

"I don't usually do this kind of work," Brenda, a biologist I know, said when she left a message on my phone. "But I found a dead possum that you might like and threw it in the refrigerator for you." When I told Brenda and others that I was going to make a banjo and needed animal hide, they got carried away. A neighbor stopped me on the way to the post office with directions to a dead squirrel on the side of the road, and a friend delivered news of his latest decomposing find to me as I sat at a crowded lunch table. Pretty soon people in three counties were pulling off the road and tossing carcasses in the back of their cars—for Harvey. "Every time I see roadkill," my friend John told me, "I think of you."

When the dogs brought a mangled groundhog to my porch, I knew that it was time to put an end to the scavenger hunt and asked Dick Aunspaugh—an artist with an abiding love of Native American lore—to help me make a rawhide top for my homemade banjo. He suggested deer.

Dick had picked up the hide at a local slaughterhouse and when I arrived was already fleshing out the inside with a tool, fat and goo falling away as he scraped toward himself. "You have to bring the tool straight toward you," he said, handing the blade to me. "Go too far this way or that," he added, moving his hand like a loose rudder, "and the skin will tear." My gestures were timid—I probably would have thrown up if I had thought about what I was doing—and when

I reached the teat of the doe and scraped right over it I did wince and get a little queasy.

Later we stretched the skin across a rack and leaned it against a teepee made from oak trunks. It was a beautiful fall day—windy with a bright blue sky, the mountains around us choked with autumnal colors and the lawn littered with yellows and reds. "It should dry in a few hours out here," Dick said while giving the hide one more scraping, the juice from the skin running off the blade into the grass.

It wasn't until the next day, though, that we got to work again, and by this time the hide had turned a light brown, streaked here and there with dark colors. "Blood," Dick said—some apparently remains in the blue-white skin even after repeated scrapings. We turned the rack over and began to shave the fur away from the top with another blade, this one set to cut at a right angle with the hide. "This is the dry-scraping method," Dick said, "the one used by Indians in tribes all across America."

As I scraped away, trying to see a banjo in all this, Dick pointed to a hole in the shoulder of the hide. "See? The hunter must have been in a tree stand, up above." A bullet like that would make a mess of an animal's insides, I thought watching Dick trace the trajectory of the bullet across the skin. "Look," he said, holding up the opposite edge, exposing a hole the size of a fist ripped into the tough flesh. "It blew out here."

A banjo is more like a wonder of nature than a musical instrument, in the same league as panther, lightning bolt, and tornado. Like a mountain, it has no will of its own and succumbs to no one. Like a creek, it makes the same noise over and over and never repeats itself. Like the wind, it changes what it finds and leaves nothing behind. It does only what it does and that is always too much. Cussedly limited, it follows the path of most resistance, creating music from the sparks.

It is hysterical. Those who hear only happiness in its jangle—and see black-faced minstrels or hillbillies or bewhiskered beatniks when they hear the name—mistake its hysteria for happiness. It asks ears to bear all that fingers can do, and when the fingers stop and the banjo is safely back in its case, what it has done rings on in the ears, the limping and thumping of its clawhammer beat nestling deep in the body and, in due time, becoming one with the lub-dub and whoosh of restless and ailing hearts.

Next to writing, the banjo is the hardest skill I have ever learned. For twenty-five years a banjo that my father bought for me when I was a boy had leaned unused against the wall in my closet, a mystery, a bedevilment. Most of the problem was lack of time—I was busy earning a living and raising a family and the banjo was low on the list of things to do. The rest of the problem was that the licks—the motions of the right hand—did not come naturally to me, probably because I play the guitar.

The basic pick on the guitar is down and up—down with the thumb and up with the fingers. With the banjo, the clawhammer stroke is all down—a bit like shaking water off of your fingers—and, probably toughest of all for the guitarist who leads with the thumb, the banjo player leads with the nail of the index finger, picking out melodies, the thumb, coming down last in the sequence, an afterthought.

Those years of playing the guitar had ruined me in another way. Unlike the guitar, the highest string on the banjo is set beside the lowest, so when I picked the instrument up it seemed upside down, no matter how I held it, and when I played—or tried to—I felt as if I were doing a headstand. Oddly, walking while playing seemed to help, especially if

I side-shuffled to the left in a vain attempt to move the instrument where the fingers would not go, but that was a little too comic, me playing the same chord over and over and walking out the back door and across the yard, ending up somewhere near the trash cans and smiling apologetically to neighbors driving by. So, time after time, I put the damn thing away in disgust.

While the banjo sat, propped against the wall and ignored behind the pantlegs in my closet, I would still listen enviously to banjo music and hear the controlled stumbling of its rhythms in my head. A few times—I remember this distinctly—I dreamed the fingering, over and over all night, doing it perfectly in sleep, and upon waking, drawn irresistibly to the back of my closet, yanked the cursed thing out of its spot, tuned the old strings, and, in broad daylight, tried again. Each time, after these dreams, I almost had it, my tongue crawling out of the corner of my mouth as I tried to get the fingers to do my will, but sooner or later I began to lean to the left and, after a few bars, had a funny feeling that if I kept on like this my head would fall off.

There is really no other sound like the clawhammer, and for this I guess we should be grateful. It is called clawhammer because the hand is curved and fingers extended in a way similar to a hammerhead, the name suggesting a brittle, constricted movement. To me, the hand looks more like a scampering rabbit, an undulation with a kink in it. The kink is the first downstroke, the nail of the forefinger hitting the string, the hare leaping over fallen trees while other notes scamper along ignominiously behind, all hindquarters and scurrying legs. To learn how to play I would slow the stroke to an agonizing tortoise crawl, methodically going through the motions. Imagine sex that is all foreplay, the rhythm of the bodies never catching up with the breathing of the lovers. It was frustrating.

Then one day it clicked. I have to admit I had been practicing with the usual ludicrous results, but success came, as it often does, when I stopped trying. I was sitting in my office after a day of teaching, grading papers in silence, when I looked up and knew I could do it. Something snapped—some old guitar string of the mind—and the clawhammer, even many of its variations, was suddenly available to me, and I could play it standing stock still. Even now, after years of successfully keeping my head on as I play, I am so happy it is hard to repress a smile.

> As a boy I recall going along with Dad to the woods to get the timber for banjo-making. He selected a tree by its appearance and by sounding . . . hitting a tree with a hammer or axe broad-sided, to tell by the sound if it's straight-grained.
>
> —Frank Proffitt

It wasn't long after I got the hang of playing the banjo that I decided to make one. I went into the woods behind my house and considered the possibility: a banjo cut from a tree by my favorite creek. I even banged on a few trunks with a hammer, the clang echoing off the hills around me. "I can't describe it in words," Frank Proffitt once said, "but I see inside the tree by the sound of hitting it." Well, *I* couldn't see a thing. No matter how many times I banged the trunk, the bark remained inscrutable. Soon I gave up. I had never felled a tree before, and visions of being pinned under an enormous poplar kept me from trying.

My next plan was to go to a lumber mill, but after visiting three mills in North Carolina, I gave up on that idea, too. These places were doing big jobs—with eighteen-wheelers hauling out flats of hardwood lumber for furniture makers. No one had time for a lone banjo. "I'd have to stop these jobs and reset the saw to give you a finished piece," the manager of the third mill told me. "We can't do that till dinner." He spat on the gravel parking lot, and we both looked together in silence at the gray tree line and a sky as dull and colorless as galvanized metal. Things were looking glum, and he could sense, I guess, my disappointment. Behind us the saw never stopped grinding. "Hell," he added at last, looking around to be sure no one could hear. "They sell the stuff at Lowe's."

So I collected the poplar for my authentic banjo by sounding the wood at the discount hardware store. I stood for an hour or more at the display eyeing the long boards for the neck and checking the grain on the wide boards that would make up the body. I bought other supplies there—stain, brass screws, and drill bits—saving the best for last. I had read that most homemade banjos had a six-inch skin head because the skin had to be fitted over a standard piece of stovepipe. Sure enough, stovepipe—in many lengths—could be found in the wood-burner section of the hardware store, all of it with six-inch diameters. After a day of gathering supplies, I had all that I needed and headed home, over the mountain, a banjo—or most of it at least—clattering unshaped and unbuilt in the trunk of my car.

> My earliest memory was of waking up on a wintry morning and hearing my father picking . . . in a slow mournful way.
> —Frank Proffitt

The patron saint of the mountain banjo is Frank Proffitt. There are, of course, several contenders for the position, since the mountains from Georgia to West Virginia have produced many great traditional banjo players—Buell Kazee, Bascom Lunsford, Clarence Ashley, Samantha Bumgardner, and Hedy West to name a few—but Proffitt, who played the songs on a banjo he made, sang with such simplicity and directness, such dignity, that it broke your heart. If saints can come bearing wood, hide, and catgut, then Proffitt was one.

He was born and raised in Beech Mountain, North Carolina, an area that was once rich in songs and music making. His life was isolated. His father, Wiley Proffitt, never saw a city until he was middle-aged. Frank didn't, either, until he was fourteen and, with friends, hiked to Mountain City, Tennessee. It was, by and large, a life insulated from the modern American experience. "I reckon you might call me a loner," Proffitt once admitted. Sometimes he would spend the entire day in the cabin near his house that served as workshop and retreat. "I like people, you understand, but I look forward to coming here to the old house where I make the banjos. . . . It gives me time to think."

It was in the cabin, while he was working, that the lyrics of songs, carried in his memory on the voices of his father and others like Noah Proffitt and Aunt Nancy Proffitt, would come to him, hundreds and hundreds of tunes, most of which can be traced back to ancient English ballads. Others, such as "Tom Dooley," grew out of local legends and lore. Some of his earliest memories included sitting on the hearth by the fire listening to the adults in his family tell tales and sing. Most of what he knew about music he learned from them, especially his father, a man Proffitt described as "always busy but never hurrying."

Frank Warner, singer and song collector, brought Proffitt's music to a larger world. Together he and the mountain singer went to the Folk Festival at the University of Chicago. There Proffitt heard bluegrass pickers using a flashy Scruggs picking style, and he had to resist the temptation to change the way he played. "I'd be myself," he thought, "and if they liked it fine. If they didn't, well, I would just come on back here to the mountains and forget the whole thing." Sandy Paton, who recorded Proffitt's songs, once asked him what he thought of Scruggs's picking. "I'd like to be able to do it," Proffitt said, "and then not do it."

What he did do—it was his holy calling—was remain faithful to the tradition of singing and banjo playing he inherited. "I know I'm not much, musically speaking," he said once. "I do what I am able, trying to keep to the original as handed me from other days." By being himself and nothing more, Proffitt claimed his inheritance, taking his place in a lineage that bound him to "other days"—a heritage that carried him back, as certainly as the genes in his blood, to the first song, a continuous, evolving tradition passed from the lips of one person to the ears of another, the songs, as old as the human race, arriving as naturally as the color of eyes and hair.

Like sex, the banjo has a capacity for sadness commensurate with its reputation for fun. Banjo songs often tell the tale of women who vow never to give their pleasure "to another gamblin' man" and men who "dug" on a grave "the best part of last night" to bury the women they killed. Songs like "Little Matty Groves" and "The Twa Sisters" offer up grizzly stories of love and revenge while the banjo's fifth string plunks merrily along.

In some ways, "The Cuckoo"—one of the oldest banjo tunes—is the most eerie, telling a tale with adulterous overtones of a bird that "sings as she flies" and lays eggs in the nests of others, our word cuckold coming from the name of the notorious bird. "The Cuckoo" is about many kinds of losses with the usual culprits: spent desire, gaudy temptations, and dreamy places. The chorus about the "pretty bird," the constant in all versions of the song, is linked with verses about gambling and leaving home, ways that life slips through our greedy grasp.

The banjo is for losers. It followed slaves from Africa—the earliest written reference is from Granger's 1794 slave narrative *Sugar Cane,* which mentions "the wild banshaw's melancholy sound"—and became the meeting place for the disenfranchised of Africa and Europe when blacks and blackfaced minstrels brought the banjo to the Appalachians. The perfect mate for the fiddle, it added a steady, syncopated rhythm to the plaintive melodies of poor farmers of English and Scottish descent who had settled in the southern mountains. It was played by lonely and homesick soldiers on both sides during the Civil War and later was enlisted in the labor battles of the thirties and civil rights protests in the sixties.

The fifth string, the "ring" of the banjo, makes the instrument sound lively, but in a minor tuning or on a homemade mountain banjo the ring sours to a whine rising clear and unchanging above the low groan of ordinary woes. It is the plaintive call of lost innocence, a giggling girl brought down panting on the loamy wood's floor, her cry, muffled in the shaggy darknesses of pine and oak, rising above the tree line only to die on thin air.

> The shavings and smell of fresh wood, the going alone to the woods to get the wood . . . the tuning up for the first time the new banjo, will always be good memories for me.
>
> —Frank Proffitt

I found the pattern for my banjo in *Foxfire* magazine—the magazine about mountain lore published by high school students in Rabun County, not far from where I live. I adapted the plan used by Stanley Hicks, who, like Proffitt, lives on Beech Mountain in North Carolina. My banjo had a small skin head and fretless neck and followed an old design that Hicks had learned from his father.

There is, in fact, a photograph in the book of one of his father's banjos, one that goes back to the thirties or forties, no doubt. The tailpiece is askew and tattered, the wood wormy, and the head damaged in places—rotting along the metal edge where the stovepipe rubs against the skin. Still, in the photograph the banjo is strung and could, probably, have been played. It is the prototype of mine. I made changes, of course, putting in brass screws for the tailpiece and taking the tuning pegs from the banjo my father had given me, but most of the rest followed Hick's design. I bought poster board to draw the pattern—the long neck and the three circles for the body of the instrument. I cut these out, taped them to the wood, and, with a pencil, carefully transferred the design. I watched the banjo take shape under my hands.

I broke a jigsaw blade and nearly ruined the saw trying to cut my wood. The problem was mine. The saw had been a gift from my father-in-law, and I didn't think to oil it. So I ground through most of the project with blue smoke pouring out of the machine.

Silence and humming and whistling are built into my banjo, because a lot of that was going on as I designed and measured the instrument. But I have to admit that pure and damnable noise was built in too, the grind of the jigsaw blade, not to mention a string of curses, at times drowning out all other sounds, creating a roaring place which drove anything pretty out of earshot and embedded a noisy residue—I'm sure—into the grain of the poplar.

I cut the pieces for my banjo one at a time over the course of a day or two, laying them out on the Ping-Pong table as I went. The neck came in two thin pieces, one more than two feet long, the other a short back support. The body was made up of three circles about ten inches wide and less than an inch thick—these would be screwed together with an opening at the top for the neck. I couldn't resist at each stage putting the rough-cut pieces together just to see what the banjo would look like and, holding it, *feel* like in my lap. The last cut, the hardest, was the scrolled headpiece, the part that seems so out of place on this box of sticks and skin, the curl in the pompadour of a country boy's hair, a quick way to fancy.

I spent a week sanding all the pieces by hand, rubbing them down to a steady beat that echoed and complemented the heartbeat and anticipated the plunky dactylic rhythm to come from the banjo—bum-*dit*ty, bum-*dit*ty, bum-*dit*ty. When I finished I gave the instrument a light stain, screwed all the parts together, and proudly showed it to a friend.

"It's great," she said. "When are you going to sand it?"

So back to sanding again, turning to an electric sander this time, which left the "bum-*dit*ty" of sandpaper in the sawdust, but ending again by hand until the wood was powdery soft and ready for the stain. All of this was new to me, and I thought—at each step of the way—that the project could fail, giving me little but some oddly shaped kindling for my effort. I got so finicky near the end that I redid the stain four times, resanding each time, before I got it right. I varnished over and over, in an attempt to get a coat that was nearly perfect, without bubbles or streaks, holding my breath each time in a kind of prayer until I was done.

"The aggravating thing about a homemade banjo," a friend told me, "is that you are forever tuning it." Made from hide and wood, the mountain banjo changes with the barometer, and because the ingredients were once alive it is always in some stage of degeneration, rotting in the picker's arms. There is a shuffle and ache in the sound worthy of the weak and vulnerable and broken: the barefooted thumpety-thump of a baby charging into its first steps; the hobbled, three-legged gait of the old man, doubled over his cane, making his solitary way to the post office. Unlike a store-bought banjo, the homegrown version has a life of its own and is perpetually dying.

A homemade banjo is pitched lower than a manufactured one, so the high-pitched fifth string is not bright, but soft and plunky, a ringing emptiness, a drone pitched just high enough to be felt more than heard. Like a semicolon it clears a space; the rest of the notes, stopping short, stumble to get around it. Each style—frailing, drop thumb, and double thumb—must accommodate the drone, the way you might favor a hurt knee: limping and wincing, making it to the other side of the room by grabbing chair backs along the way.

It is possible—no one knows for sure—that the ancient Greek lyre was tuned much like a mountain banjo, with a high-pitched drone, called the *paranêté,* the "opposite" or "side" string. "Greek lyres," the musicologist Curt Sachs speculated, may have tuned to the same notes as the *kerâr,* an African lyre with a skin drum, having the "the same peculiar arrangement with the high string closest to the lowest one of an ascending scale," which is, he adds, "like the modern banjo." Anyone who plays a homemade banjo, or hears Frank Proffitt play and sing murder ballads like "Bo Lampkin," knows that this sound could go back to the Greek of Homer, ancient songs of hanged women and gored heroes.

With a banjo we are never more than a note away from woe. Unlike the guitar and other stringed instruments, the banjo uses many different tunings. If, in the key of G, we tune one string up a half tone, all the joy goes out of the banjo, replaced by a haunting clatter like wind in poplars. This sad stutter is the original call of the banjo and goes by several names; "mountain minor" and "sawmill tuning" are two. It is a modal tuning, not unlike the notes of ancient aeolian harps. It is the tuning of the wind. When I crank up the second string, something gives in the box, and when I get the tuning set and play, the banjo whimpers, a limp lodged in the rhythm. It breaks your heart.

In mountain minor the intervals between the strings are close—the notes all bunched—the overlap creating empty places or holes in the sound, making any continuous line of music, even a simple melody, difficult. The minor key is so insistent that the tune simply wanders off, shaking its head, leaving nothing but the haunting repetition of a few harmony notes. Singing a tune in mountain minor is like trying to tell your life's story above the back-and-forth stroke of the saw, a moaning that has nothing to do with the tale except that it sets the voice free, the words riding a sound as melancholy as hardwood, hide, and gut—all that came to the hand of the banjo maker and did not get away.

It is this sadness, this ache, that renders the mountain banjo beautiful, beautiful primarily for what it lacks. There is no bluegrass in it at all. Played in the clawhammer style or double thumbed, it is soft, like the rustle of pantlegs in tall grasses. Picks are traded up for mere fingertips and, at every note, string leaves flesh reluctantly, with a moan.

> When the strings was tuned and the musical notes began to fill the cabin . . . I looked upon my father as the greatest man on earth for creating such a wonderful thing out of a piece of wood, a greasy skin, and some strings.
>
> —Frank Proffitt

The hardest part of making a banjo is waiting for the skin head to dry. There is no way of knowing whether or not the homemade banjo "rings" until the drum is set in place. It is the first true test. Once that is done, and the wet hide allowed to harden overnight, the maker can tell with a mere thump if he has a banjo or a pile of polished lumber.

I began by cutting a circle of deerhide and wetting it in the sink—the skin getting soft, nearly gooey, under my hands, but tough and durable still. I stapled the skin into the wooden body so that it hung loosely in place, cringing, I admit, with each staple, and when I finished and held the banjo up to the light the skin sagged like a windless sail. After several tries I cut the stovepipe so that it would fit nicely into the body, making a strong, resonant frame for the skin. I put a wire about the stovepipe to keep it from stretching out of shape and ended by screwing the base to the top, securely holding the stovepipe in place. The drumhead took shape, tightening over the stovepipe with only a little slack. I set my banjo in our living room on the tall oak secretary, a piece of furniture built by my great-great grandfather, and hoped for the best.

A banjo needs a warm room to dry properly, preferably a room heated by a fireplace. A friend who grew up in the mountains where I live tells me that when families would gather to sing, the banjo player always wanted to be near the fire. "On rainy nights, these old players would unpack their banjos and hold them up to the flames so that the top would dry." The party did not begin until the banjo player drummed the banjo head and announced, "That's about right."

As the head on my banjo dried overnight on the secretary, the windows whitened with eerie light and the banjo filled with silence and moonlight becoming a strange wonder of nature. The next day when I took it down from its perch, the moon-white, mottled drumhead was dry. I heard, in some distant clearing of my mind, songs about love and death and whiskey and going far, far away. I heard the distant cry of a cuckoo singing on the wing. I hesitated to touch the drum, afraid it would break, afraid too that it would sound dead, but as I ran my hand along the top I felt that it had grown taut and rock-hard, and, when I tapped it with a finger, it thumped like a heart—not *my* heart, it was too wild and odd to call my own, but a heart nonetheless, and I loved it.

Soldier's Joy

During lunch I took my banjo down to Cupid's Falls and played "Soldier's Joy" to the roar of tumbling water. Cupid's is a small waterfall adjacent to the campus where I teach and is aptly named for all the young lovers from the college who make their way there at night. I often come on sunny spring days toting my banjo and a bag lunch, and sit on the concrete abutment that juts out to the edge of the waterfall. Under a canopy of dogwood—all green and white—I play and sing, with sunlight glittering on the grass and rocks and churning water all around me. It's nearly heaven.

"Soldier's Joy" is a fiddle tune that fits the strings of a banjo perfectly. During the Civil War it went by several names. "Love Somebody," "Sweet Sixteen," and "Payday in the Army" are a few of the titles, all suggesting a soldier's joys. The tune has the Ionian lilt of free time about it and a happy ring as well, like a handful of loose change in a young man's pocket. The Skillet Lickers from Atlanta made it famous, and Clayton McMichen introduced it in his 1929 recording with an invitation to dancers. "I want you to grab that girl, shake her foot, and moan."

There was no girl to grab on this mossy bank, and I don't dance, but I did tap my foot, and while I played—oblivious to all but beauty and joy—a little blue butterfly flipped-flopped through the air over my left shoulder, a happy if befuddled harbinger of spring. I often see these blue butterflies when I work outdoors and remember once when two of them fluttered about my head for most of an afternoon while I mowed the lawn. They seem to like people, and I fooled myself into thinking that this one, dipping and tumbling in front of me while I played, was dancing to my tune, another fresh recruit set free by "Soldier's Joy." We carried on that way through the A and B sections of the tune, the butterfly gamboling to my syncopations and the heady rush of churning water over rocks. I smiled and I imagined—somehow!—that the butterfly was smiling too.

But when I stopped the butterfly did not, and in its flutterings I realized a sad fact that biologists have been telling poets for some time now. It is a mistake to read human emotions into the natural world. Insects are not sad or happy in the way we are—no matter what our poets say. They do not dance to our tunes. There are no soldiers in this butterfly's world, and joy has to go in quotation marks. The butterfly was not dancing to the tune at my fingertips but to the sun, the warmth, and the prospect of nectar and copulation. The butterfly was tumbling to the tune of tumbling waters.

But so, I realized, was I, and at that moment I saw—and felt, as if for the first time—a happy truth, hidden in a sobering fact, a truth that binds us all and sets us free. My fingers had been dancing to the rhythm of tumbling waters, too. I had merely stopped dancing for a while to do some fuzzy thinking; otherwise, I was as much a participant in the butterfly's dance as it was in mine. I struck up the tune again, and the butterfly didn't skip a beat. We returned to our frolicking ways. I was sweet sixteen, it was payday, and I loved everybody! The butterfly was not dancing to my fingers, to be sure, but both of us moved in consort nonetheless, dancing to the tumble and roar of the undying song of the universe.

The Mixolydian Mode

Sorghum shows its tassels in the Mixolydian mode, and play ripens into courtship—often imperceptibly at first. In the Mixolydian song "Pretty Betty Martin" a boy first admires Betty's dancing—"Lord, she could tip-toe fine"—but the next time he sees her the man he has become is ready for more than play: "Stand back, boys," he announces, "this one's mine!"

Mixolydian is the mode of consummation, when young men achieve full height and the curves of a woman create a waist that will break the fifth string on any man's banjo. Play is transformed by the erotic tug of sex into lovemaking, though our songs have no terms but the language of play to talk about the change. "Swing that young girl up and down the holler," the song says euphemistically. "Swing her up on her tippy, tippy, toes."

In this mode, sometimes called bagpipe tuning, the top and bottom strings of the dulcimer are tuned to the same note an octave apart. The result is a happy jangle, a giddy ringing that stirs the heart. "You can," says the dulcimer player Kevin Roth, "start the scale anywhere," making this the promiscuous tuning, so easy to play that anything goes.

In the Mixolydian mode boys in my town with hair slicked back and a hitch in their step follow a red ribbon and bouncing curls onto the dance floor of the old middle school gym, stomping all the while to the words of a caller. With built-in wooden bleachers on each side, the gym houses a basketball court, marked off for fouls and out-of-bounds, but on dance nights the floor serves as a stomping place and being out of bounds is the point.

In the Mixolydian mode young lovers follow a ribbon of sound that winds its way above the droning generations. When the music starts, they let go of their partners, who move—spinning, twirling, up on tiptoes and at times lifted high into the air—into the hands and arms of others but, when the music stops, find themselves, breathless and sweating, in the arms of the one who will take them home.

The Devil by Surprise

Day and night our porch has its own music: the rise and fall of voices softened by outdoors, the cymbal crash of children charging by, the clicking of insects in the grass, the fluted call of a cardinal in the woods, the bark and ballyhoo of dogs keeping opossum, coon, bear, and other silent, red-eyed foragers at bay on into the evening, and the settling back, once that is done, into the adagio hours after others have gone to bed and the sinister snap and crackle of the woods is muffled in night's velvet cases. This is the familiar score, punctuated, occasionally, by the cawing of crows, but tonight, as Barbara and I sit on the porch talking, I hear none of it. This summer the old men of the woods—the seventeen-year locusts—have returned. Unpacking their fiddles they send up a slow-rising drone drowning out all else. What, they ask, as the noise rises imperceptibly from a whisper to a roar in a seemingly endless syllable, are you waiting for?

We were waiting, I guess, for Nessa to come home—and had plans to buy her, at last, a fiddle. The locusts, gestating silently for most of her life, had come alive and sawed and clacked and made a racket while Barbara and I discussed the possibility. Nessa was returning for the summer months after her first year in college. She had always loved music and dancing and singing of all sorts, including clogging and other purely mountain forms of carrying on. Now, heralded by the drone of cicadas, she was on her way back to the mountains, and a fiddle seemed like a nice way to welcome her home.

At the local Radio Shack, which doubles as a music store in our town, I eyed a homemade violin with oversized, handmade pegs and a flat finish, but Rachel Caviness, a friend whose orchestral violin never got in the way of her fiddling, shook her head, saying that it would be hard for an *expert* to play that. She handed me a conventional violin which, she argued, might end up being more than a wall hanging. When Nessa arrived it was waiting for her, in the room that Barbara had fixed up for her return, sitting in a case on her bed. It rested on her quilted cover, making a pretty picture, and we can, I suppose, be forgiven for getting nostalgic. We had forgotten, seeing it so innocently displayed, that where I live the fiddle has always been called the devil's instrument.

No one knows for sure why it is called that. Fiddle music inevitably leads to dancing—that is probably the source of its bad reputation in the mountains, where, for generations, dancing was frowned upon by the godly. Our word *fiddle* comes from *fithele* in Old English and was spelled many ways—*fithel, fydill,* and *fyddel* are three—before it settled down in the late sixteenth century to the spelling we now know, *fiddle.* It can be traced back to the name of the Sabine goddess of joy and victory, Vitula, who was celebrated, appropriately enough, in pagan cult practices in the days before Rome. No doubt there was a good deal of un-Christian dancing and partying going on then, as well.

Fiddles are violins, part of a family of instruments that should not be confused with their distant cousins, the viols. The two families of instruments were in fact rivals, violins playing second fiddle during the seventeenth century to the more popular lira and viola da gamba. "The violin is too crude," the author of *Harmonie universelle* wrote in 1636. The "use of the violin had bin litle in England except by comon fiddlers," a lawyer in the court of Charles II wrote. But even as these disparaging remarks were being made, Nicolo Amati, the famous violin maker, and his young apprentice Antonio Stradivari had begun creating the elegant design that would make the violin the orchestra's premier instrument.

Nessa's violin, ordinary in every way, follows the design of these Italian masters. Small improvements have been made since their days. The neck of the modern violin is slightly longer and the interior structure stronger. The bridge is curved so that the violinist will hit only one string at a time—an improvement that some mountain fiddlers rectify by whittling the bridge flat so that they can hit several strings at once. These changes, whether resisted or not, are minor. Once the design was established some four hundred years ago, the violin changed very little, so that the instrument that Nessa put under her chin the day we gave it to her is very much like that played by Corelli and Vivaldi.

The bow is another matter. Originally it was shaped like the weapon it was named for, giving the performer a martial look. In the eighteenth century the concave bow made its debut, all of the tension of the original bow rendered compact, the power elegantly hidden away. This is the bow that crossed the Atlantic when settlers came to America. Shorter than the modern bow, which was not created until the nineteenth century, it was perfect for the choppy strokes of mountain music, a style of playing that is often disparaged in our time as the improper execution of the long bowing motion of the modern orchestral violin. In fact, the short bow strokes heard in the hills came first, and characterized the bowing movements of good old boys like Haydn and Mozart.

The fiddle made its way into my area with the original white settlers in the 1800s. They brought their old-world violins, with the short bow and flatter bridge—and their fiddle songs too. The fiddle was portable—a boon for someone traveling light—and, until the banjo was introduced in the late nineteenth century, it was the only instrument in most mountain households. Over the generations, the songs, and their titles, evolved. In *Tennessee Strings* Charles Wolfe writes that the most famous fiddle tune of all, "Turkey in the Straw," was originally an old English song called "The Jolly Miller," and "Bonaparte Crossing the Rhine" became, by a twist of historical amnesia, "Bonaparte's Retreat Across the Rocky Mountains" and "Sherman's March to the Sea."

And yet, despite time and distance and little written record, the melodies are remarkably like the originals, and many eighteenth-century titles, such as "Soldier's Joy" and "Fisher's Hornpipe," remain unchanged. In 1909 Louise Rand Bascom wrote about a fiddler in his nineties who began performances by stating that he was playing "his great-great grandfather's 'pieces.'" The songs were respected—they were part of each family's heritage—so innovation was discouraged, the isolation of the Appalachians acting as a check on change.

In the nineteenth century fiddling contests sprang up in little towns all through the mountains and were popular enough to swing several elections. There is the story of John W. Tibbatts, who, according to B. A. Botkin in *A Treasury of Southern Folklore,* won the hearts of his constituents in Tennessee because he played a fine fiddle with his left hand, only to lose the election when his opponent, W. W. Southgate, claimed that Tibbatts played even better right-handed. Tibbatts could "bend the trees with his sweet tunes," Southgate admitted, but he refused to lower himself by doing so for ordinary people, "whom," Southgate added, "he thinks jackasses." The better fiddler lost.

Not true in another Tennessee election called the "War of the Roses." Two brothers, Bob and Alf Taylor, battled it out politically and musically to be governor of the state in 1886. Cartoons in northern magazines showed them sitting on the stage playing fiddles with roses tossed at their feet. Bob Taylor, the better musician, "fiddled his way to fame" as one local newspaperman wrote. He knew that many in his audience saw the fiddle as the "devil's box" and took a calculated risk when he decided to campaign with it. He was, of course, accused of "fiddling around" with the issues. But he won, and never forgot the role that the fiddle played in his victory. "Politicians sneered at me as a fiddler," he admitted in an open letter to his constituents, "but the girls said it was no harm, and the boys voted while I fiddled, and the fiddle won."

Nessa and her teacher, the musician J. D. Robinson, had contests of their own. At her first lesson J. D. asked her to balance her bow on her toe and hold it there as long as possible. "The fiddler has to stay balanced," J. D. explained to her, and I thought of the times that I had seen mountain fiddlers standing still on the stage at dances, nothing moving but the arm, while everyone swirled around them. The true fiddler sways, leaning in when he dwells on a note and tilting back on his heels for a wide open passage, wavering like the bow on Nessa's toe when, in front of the refrigerator, she demonstrated her first lesson for me. Any movement at the tip of the bow has to be compensated for by the motion of the foot, the whole held in balance until the tune winds down and the fiddler releases the last note with a jerk, opening his arms wide and stepping back from the mike.

"The art of playing the fiddle," says Charlie Acuff, who grew up in the famous Tennessee music family, "is in the bow." The bow shapes the sound, so that fiddle music, like sentences, comes in phrases. It is this—the ability to phrase a continuous sound—that sets the fiddle apart. Other mountain instruments are plucked or picked—even the bass is generally thumped and slapped by the player. The fiddler alone takes a line of music, like a ribbon, and threads it endlessly through the song, the phrasing doing for the ear what the ribbon does for the eye: catching it with brightness, holding it in its curlicues, and letting it get lost in tangled luxury. Like the ribbon, too, this thread of sound can take our breath away, the giggle produced on the strings becoming by turns and without cease a whine and a moan and a cry—the devil's instrument indeed.

The "Devil rides upon a Fiddlesticke," Shakespeare wrote, and mountain people say "thick as fiddlers in hell," so it naturally follows that the best way to learn the fiddle is, as one story has it, to "go to the graveyard with it and start practicin'." Botkin tells the tale of a boy who had his first—and last—fiddle lesson in the cemetery. Sitting among the gravestones, he struck up "Old Dan Tucker," the devil's tune and "the first thing he will learn you to play." No sooner did he start than he heard a noise, "bangity bang," and stopped. The boy had heard stories of ghosts taking the form of steam in graveyards and hogs seeing the wind—it looks "just as red as blood." Afraid, he calmed himself by playing some more. Again he heard the noise—bangity bang—and felt steam on his face. He dropped his fiddle and ran, glad to leave the instrument behind, thinking that "the ghosts could practice on it all they wanted."

The temptation to quit is mighty.

Not long after Nessa had her lesson, she and I were on the porch attempting our first tune together—an inauspicious, if not downright dismal, beginning. Every third stroke of the bow, one or both of us would cringe. The parakeet, which sings to street noise, fell silent. Dogs left the porch. The rose withered. Nessa is a natural musician, and I thought she would be up and playing in a day or two, but the fiddle had other ideas. "Turkey in the Straw" came out just turkeys and "Chicken in the Bread Pan Scratchin' at the Dough" mere scratchin', the old titles taking on a new meaning. We both settled into the porch swing when we were done, she grumpy and my smile a little brittle.

Eventually, though, the lessons—and the instrument itself—began to teach her, her fingers falling to the notes that her ear said were right. The bowing became more natural, uniform, controlled. We were still a long way from the expressive and freewheeling fiddle magic we heard in our minds, but we were having fun, the fiddle notes dancing out of the instrument—well, stumbling, perhaps, but giddy like new lovers off to the woods—and we ended our times on the porch with smiles.

"Fiddlesticks!" we say. The word begins with a deceptively soft consonant but soon gives way to a bundle of short *i*'s wrapped up in *d*'s and *t*'s and *k*'s. Three syllables long, it naturally wants to divide into several accents, but when we are angry or sarcastic, which we usually are when we say it, we load all of the emphasis on the beginning. *Fid*dlesticks! It is a handy declaration for taking the air out of politicians, undoing the nonsense of teenagers, and making children laugh.

The word *fiddlesticks* tells most of the story, but the essence of the fiddle is in the happy redundancy "fiddle around." *Fiddle* by itself suggests meandering and floating, but *around* renders the phrase thoroughly desultory. "Fiddle around" has come to mean play—play without aim or purpose, usually the kind that is contemptible to everyone but the players. When the fiddle starts, someone, somewhere, raises an eyebrow and frowns.

Fiddlers *do* play, creating within a limited but unpredictable range of possibility. In the days when dancing was forbidden in mountain households, fiddle songs like "Skip to My Lou" accompanied games at parties, instead of dances. As a result, the fiddle—along with its partner, the banjo—has long been associated with being refractory and lazy. The music marks off a kingdom where leisure reigns. In fact, the favorite spot for the fiddle and the banjo has been—as it is now for Nessa and me—the porch, which is conveniently located between house and field, two areas of work.

But if the fiddle is play, it is love-play. Adults pair off when the music begins—and often head for the woods together before it is done. One ancient ancestor of the fiddle—the Vienna lira kept in the Kunsthistorischer Museum—bears in Greek a happy inscription that translates as "Song is the doctor to the pains of man" and carved in the wood of the instrument's back is the doleful face of a bearded patriarch whose forehead, upon closer inspection, is made up of women's breasts. The instrument, which may have been played at one time by Leonardo da Vinci, brings the beloved and fate together in the player's arms.

Sex and sound have been linked, I suppose, since our beginnings. "Buy our cassette," one local musician tells his audience with a wink. "It is probably the only safe way to take home a musician." The taboo against mountain women playing the fiddle—an unspoken rule enforced until recently—was probably sexual as well. "The fact that mountain women—even with talent—were reluctant to touch the instrument in their men's presence," writes Charles Wolfe, "is suggestive of the curious relationship between sexual gender and folk music." *In their men's presence*—that is the phrase that counts here, the instrument and bow charged, phallic and primal.

Like play and sex, the fiddle takes us where we haven't been with what little we have. On late summer nights at our place, when the locusts calm down, the tree frogs begin their mournful clatter. A shirring fiddle sound, softer and less insistent than the moan of the cicadas, it rises and falls somnolently day and night in southern woods. It is, I've heard, a mating call, the frogs that sing the longest winning the mate. It is, unfortunately for the frogs, also a way for predators, especially owls and bats, to locate their next meal, homing in on the sound. No wonder the call is mournful—born out of longing and fear—the fiddlers' chorale rising out of the graveyard all around us and held as long as they dare.

The body of the violin—so like the body of a woman—is lovely, an elegant sound box with little need for decoration. Even the *f*-holes along the sides are utilitarian as well as beautiful, releasing the music into the air. But at the fiddlehead the instrument forgets itself, neglecting its simple duty to shape sound out of strings and wood, and gets fancy. Clarence Rathbone, who grew up in a house by a narrow gravel road on a mountain near Bakersville, North Carolina, remembered a lion's head that his father had carved into the head of a violin, and, on the fiddle he made for himself, he carved one like it from memory. The eyes, amid crosshatched lines, are sinister and lovely, and the hooded back of the head is almost Egyptian in its elegance and shocking in its beauty.

Most violin makers, when they get to the fiddlehead, content themselves with a scroll, the shape of life, a strand of DNA set on the oblique, always repeating, never the same. It is the widening gyre of Yeats's poetry, closing on the moment and opening into eternity. Young at the tip and ancient at the source, it recapitulates life, the shape beginning as a cry of delight and ending in a whisper. *Take me away!* it shouts, and *bring me back,* the echoes softly repeat, each gesture upward and outward also heading, with a fillip and a flourish, down.

The fiddlehead is like the lightheaded, ground-bound fern that bears its name, or the whorls of the sea-choked conch, but most of all it is like the music itself that begins in the tonic, works its way up and down any melody, detours, momentarily, into a relative minor, but soon leaves that darkening behind and happily reaches a climax somewhere in the major once again, dwelling on the flurry of notes we hold our breath to hear, only to return, dazed and dizzy, battered and beatified, like us, along the curve of spent desires down to the tonic, the note we feel as home before we recognize it, the note at the core of the scroll where it all began.

The fiddle brings people together, marking off a meeting place where almost anything can happen. "Billy in the Low Ground" is a tune about a man who falls into a sinkhole and plays his fiddle to gather folks to his aid. There is also the tale, taken from *The Life of David Crockett,* about Davy and a party of travelers hearing fiddle music as they approached the Washita River. In the middle of nowhere the fiddler was playing "Hail, Columbia, Happy Land," followed by "Over the Water to Charley," in a brisk and lively way. "That's mighty mysterious," said one in Davy's party. "A notch beyant my measure," said another. When Davy suggested that they press on and find the source of the music, they came upon the fiddler atop a wagon floating down the river, the whole rig—horse and all—about to be swept away by the current. After Davy and his men saved the fiddler, they asked why, in such a dire situation, he played the fiddle. He knew he needed help, he said, and there was "nothing in univarsal nature so well calculated to draw people together as the sound of a fiddle."

"The scraping of the fiddles attracted us to the sugar house," wrote Margaret Hall, who was slumming in America in 1827 for her book *The Aristocratic Journey: Being the Outspoken Letters of Mrs. Basil Hall Written During a Fourteen Months' Sojourn in America*. While spending the night at a house in Louisiana, she heard that irresistible string of notes and, temporarily setting aside her aristocratic ways, followed the music to its source. Cleared of machinery and anything that says work, the sugarhouse was a shelter from the world, and there, in the lamplight,

Mrs. Hall discovered the melting pot, men and women dancing "a kind of Irish jog to the music of negro musicians." Needless to say, Margaret found it "very odd," especially when she was asked to join in the dance and, for the time being, became merely Maggie.

Hayesville, North Carolina, just across the border from my hometown, was renowned for its fiddle dances in the thirties. "We'd go t'hotels down there at Hayesville, big hotels, the Herbert—they had some big-uns," said Lawton Brooks to the writers of *Foxfire*. "They had the 'grapevine twist.' Boy, that'd kill you! And the Georgia 'rang tang,'" he explained, describing the dances. "Earl Anderson was the best man I ever heard t'call. He run a hardware there in Hayesville."

Hayesville is small now, with little left of its boom days as a lumber town except the tidy square at its center—and even that is much changed since the thirties. No one that I asked at the library knew about fiddle dances or the Hotel Herbert, but Jessie Martin, at the Clay County Historical Society, said there were Andersons everywhere nearby. She remembered that when she was a girl the Herberts owned a large two-story house just off the square, and she thought—since I mentioned it—that dances were once held there. Now it is a bank—no sign of the hotel anywhere—but, as I stood at the spot watching customers go in and out, I thought of fiddle music instead of tellers making change and wondered how many couples had stepped off the porch at the Herbert long ago, holding hands, fiddle music in their ears.

Dancers do not need fancy hotels, of course. "They'd dance on whatever kind of floor there was," said Sam McGee, the Grand Ole Opry star, recalling playing at dances at the beginning of the century. Sawdust or meal spread on the floor helped—"made it easier to slide." The dance would go on well past midnight, McGee and his band getting a dime per set, and by the end of an infernal night of doing the devil's work the powder would fly. "They'd have us up on a platform in the corner, and that dust would come up—your eyes would look like two burn holes in a blanket."

We still have square dances during the Sorghum Festival in my hometown, Blairsville, Georgia. Many in the town, including some bewildered visitors, gather in the old middle school gym for three Saturday nights every fall to stomp and holler. It is not a traditional square dance, I guess, since most of the time the dancers are in a huge circle, not in squares, but I have never seen so many people having so much fun. Jimmy Rogers is the caller, and John Nix plays a rosin-whitened lead fiddle for his electrified string band. The night starts quietly with a few slow numbers like "The Tennessee Waltz," but by ten o'clock the square dancers have taken over. Each song lasts up to a half hour, the crowd pleaser, of course, being "Down Yonder."

Dancers—clogging or buck dancing—pass their partners hand-to-hand or elbow-to-elbow "around the world," which is an excuse for people of all ages to hug, squeeze, or twirl friends that they nod to, politely, each day. Few sit out the dance—a woman in a wheel chair gave it a try when I was there last. At one point, dancers follow a lead couple, passing under the lifted arms of other dancers, as the line snakes around the room, moving in a pattern like the scroll on a fiddlehead, an ever tightening spiral. In my favorite trick, the leaders of this enormous line of sweaty dancers buck dance out the back door, around the gym, and back in the front door, each couple reentering with a shout, or just plain laughter, showing off their best travel-weary, high-stepping form—with a satyr in the wings and the devil, no doubt, holding open the door.

"Why should the devil have all the pretty tunes?" John Wesley once said, and it is true that in the South damnation and divinity often sound alike. The preacher Peter Cartwright tells in his autobiography about the time that he spent the night in the Cumberlands where a party was being held. When a pretty girl asked him to dance he accepted "not with some emotion, but," he admits, "with many emotions." Heading out onto the dance floor, he asked the fiddler to hold off for a moment, and taking the girl's hand, knelt down and began to pray. At first she tried to wiggle free, but soon "fell on her knees," followed by others, beginning an important revival. "I should succeed by taking the devil at surprise," Cartwright surmised, "as he has often served me."

Music is as old as sin, and the dances and games of mountain people were nothing new, even two centuries ago. They can be traced back to ancient ceremonies. One singing game called "Draw a Pail of Water" is, the musicologist Cecil Sharp writes, "a dramatic representation of several incidents connected with the ceremony of well worship." The well-known dance movement—we remember it from the game "London Bridge Is Falling Down" if nowhere else—in which a dancer passes under a canopy of arms toward the fiddler on the stage may, according to Sharp, be "an imitation of the creeping of the devotee under the sacred bush, which was frequently found by the side of the holy well." The urge is primordial and irrepressible. If there is no floor, we find a well or spring for the party site, and if there is no well or spring, we find a clearing in the woods and make a stomping ground. We have done this for ages. The fiddle merely calls us to return.

The fiddle puts time in its pocket and lets the momentary reign. If it is as young as the whir of spinning tops and children racing to the creek, it is as old as the clatter of grasshoppers and crickets in late summer afternoons, a shaky, timid cackle. The sound is timeless like the call of cicadas awkward from years of slumber, a raging that comes on so slowly and lasts so long that it seems to have no beginning or end. Late at night after others have gone to bed, I sit in the midst of the torrent, trying to locate the source of the roar all around me. I squint, my eyes playing tricks on me in the dark, and, if I am lucky, I find in the gnarled shape of trees the elbows of old men pulling down on the bow to start a set, and hear the melody—giddy, stumbling, and unsteady as the first steps of a baby—rise above the drone.

Beneath the catkins and globed fruit of an enormous hickory in the woods beside our house is a clearing. During the day it is hidden in shadows, but at night—when I walk down to it—a glow from the moon and stars and the glitter of the creek below animates it with a cool, otherworldly light. Folks used to follow fiddle sounds to a place like this, I say to myself as I scan the green, mushroom-studded circle dotted here and there with lady's slippers and jack-in-the-pulpit. On spring nights long ago they heard the wavering, fiery, and moonlit string of notes and followed the music to a circle lit by fire, where revelers arrive, feet shuffling and arms swinging, their voices sending up a shout as each new couple mingles with the bobbing throng, taking the devil by surprise.

For Nessa and me, the porch is our clearing. Here I tune the banjo while she unpacks her fiddle and rosins the bow. It may not be a holy place, if holiness has anything to do with quiet and serenity, but it is a spot set aside by our racket. I hear doors close as we tune up and windows slide shut. The dogs stand alert between us, cocking their ears expressively. Nessa usually starts off, with a note on the downstroke, and I come in behind with chords. All about us the seventeen-year locusts join in, followed by the tree frogs and their doleful love song.

It is love we are doing, all of us out there with our songs. In the face of dangers that swoop down on us in the dark, we make music. Like steam coming off the grass and blacktop after a hard summer rain, something insubstantial and real and beautiful rises among us. Midway through the song, one of us is in trouble—Nessa's face twists in consternation as a sour note shreds the mist of our music—but soon we're back in business again and a tentative smile makes its way up the corners of her mouth. I am reminded of her first lesson—balancing the bow on her toe—as her body rides the music, swaying to a rhythm that takes her far away and brings her home again.

The Dorian Mode

One mode modulates into another—that is the nature of modes. At night, after an evening of singing, friends pack up their instruments to leave, and I walk them to the cars and vans and trucks parked every which way in the drive. I wave as they pull out amid the roar of starting engines and laughter and snatches of song, and when they're gone I head back to the house—happy Mixolydian sounds still reverberating in my mind. I start to haul in chairs as evening gives way to night, when I am stopped abruptly by a whippoorwill call—a different note, the dulcimer string modulating down to the Dorian. Suddenly there is a chill in the air.

The order of the modes is not arbitrary—they are in fact related to each other, one bleeding into another in a progression as subtle and inexorable as the seasons. As surely as spring gives way to sultry, summer days, the Mixolydian mode can be made to shift, with the shifting of a note or two, to the Dorian. So many notes are shared by these two adjacent modes that the differences are incremental and insidious.

In the Dorian mode the summer days, like spent desire, drag on. The harvest moon, and the bounty it represents, has not yet rolled onto the horizon, but the honeymoon is definitely over. "Dorian mode songs," Jean Ritchie writes, "always make chills run up and down my spine," but "chill," does not seem right. There is the ringing la *note in the scale that sets this mode apart from the others, a note that normally signals joy but in the context of the other sad notes has an edge to it, a wringing sarcasm that rinses happiness out, leaving nothing but a clean, threadbare tune, like an empty cupboard or a made bed. Dorian is the mode of resentment, and resentment precedes sadness—that is the lesson of the sharpened sixth note, a shrill shattering of the minor scale. Life stings us before it hurts us—that is one way to put it—or, perhaps, we lash out before we get hurt. Who knows? Pure sadness comes later.*

In the Dorian mode the sight of a field of corn or a patch of ripe sorghum that stretches to the next hill, or fruit trees swaying gravely under a load of apples, no longer brings delight. It means work and sweat and worry. "And so much work remains to be done!" the Dorian mode, with a whine in its scale, lets us say.

There is nothing happy about this scale, which drives us, sulking, hat pulled down, into the corner, like a man after a bad day at work. There is laundry to be done, and dishes to put away, and children to haul here and there—we say, sounding that characteristically Dorian tone of complaint. On days when we are spared grief but feel no joy, when we have no energy left to play, the Dorian mode waits for us with a frown. "Oh hard is my fortune and hard is my fate," begins "Bachelor's Hall," one Dorian song. Our temptation is to retreat, a voluntary withdrawal into our own warmth, a huddled, glum, and pensive conservation of strength, because here, for the first time, our energy no longer seems boundless.

In the Dorian mode marriage feels like an erotic trap. "Controlled by my mother early and late," the woman flees to love and marriage, only to find that for the rest of her life she will be "controlled by a man." In this mode bachelor's hall seems best for both man and woman, a removal from the inexorable flow of desires that fuel the generations. Words between loved ones become bullets, carrying messages of censure and scorn. We share a bed, but only because we have to, and the man dreams of a single life where words no longer matter. "No woman to scold you, no children to boss," the grumpy voice mutters, making its way up and down the Dorian scale, lacing its sadness with the sarcasm of an occasional sweet note. "Oh happy is he who keeps bachelor's hall."

Bluing

Not long ago, I dropped into my local pawnshop to check out the banjos and guitars. As I walked in the door, two boys—well, young men—wearing camouflaged fatigues, laced boots, and military caps, their bodies crisscrossed with straps and belts, brushed past me, one of them holding a semiautomatic AK-S. They were laughing, carrying on. The one without the rifle held up his arms in shooting position and, blurting out a "da-da-da," pretended to take out all the guitars, banjos, and fiddles on the wall, his body recoiling with each shot. Eventually he took a bead on the spot between my eyes and, smiling, blew me away with a single blast—and an outburst of laughter. The other boy—the one with the gun—strutted with pride behind his friend, grinning, his head lolling from side to side in amazement. He waved at me by making a pistol with his fingers and fired with a wink.

In the mind of those boys, the store was in rubble, each musical instrument splintered and cracked, glass cases shattered, the walls pocked and cratered. I, naturally, was in a puddle of blood on the floor. When they got to the door, the first boy opened it with a flourish, bowing a little as if for royalty, while his buddy, standing grand and erect at the honor, semiautomatic weapon cradled in his arm, stepped out into high noon.

"Making the world safe for democracy," the shop owner said slyly, when the door slammed shut behind them. He shook his head as he put the money—cash—in the register, and looked up. "What can I do you out of?"

I was feeling safer already.

"Is that legal?" I wanted to ask, but I knew the answer and didn't have to ask. Around here, the right of any fool to bear arms is nearly sacred, and discussion of the subject can end in a death—usually of the pacifist. So I asked to see a guitar and kept my mouth shut.

The owner brought a small Bently for me to play. "It's real nice," he said, "just a little crack here at the bridge." He was right, the guitar was sweet, but no sooner did I touch it than I realized I didn't want to play after all. I lifted it to my knee and strummed a few chords perfunctorily. "For a hundred dollars you can take her home and fight with your wife about it," the owner joked, as he put away guns the boys did not choose.

I didn't laugh. Holding a guitar in my lap in a room full of pistols, rifles, and semiautomatic weapons, I found that the happiness, really the tenderness, I usually feel when playing any instrument was tempered by gloom. Guitars and banjos adorn one wall of my hometown pawnshop, the other wall wears guns, and—I came to feel in this sour moment—I live somewhere in the crosshairs of the contradiction.

Guns have been a part of my area—the north Georgia mountains—for as long as whites have lived here. They are the legacy of the conquerors. The most common kind of gun among settlers was the "hog" rifle, not generally used on hogs but for hunting deer, bear, and other wild game. A few hog rifles were Kentucky long rifles manufactured by German settlers in Pennsylvania, but most were homemade versions built by wily and resourceful mountain smiths.

Like their store-bought cousins, the homemade hog rifle was long, taller at times when stood on end than the hunter. Single-shot muzzle loaders, hog rifles had to be reloaded after each firing, the hunter wrapping a lead-ball bullet in a piece of greased cloth or buckskin and ramming it down the barrel. The method may seem crude, but it was far more effective than the noisy and slow "hammering technique" used on European rifles.

Most hog rifles were plain, the trigger guard and gun plate—the gun's "furniture"—made of iron, not brass, and the lean stock of walnut unadorned with metal patch-boxes and other finery. But even though they didn't look like much, hog rifles were in one way a match for their handsome cousins back East. They were deadly accurate, the combination of a long, rifled barrel, patch-protected bullet, and hunger allowing a backwoods hunter to drop a deer from a distance of two hundred yards.

For more than two centuries smiths have been making guns in the southern Appalachians, adapting to isolated conditions with creativity and know-how and passing down the traditions, usually in their families. The most famous of these gunsmithing families were the Beans, who first settled in the territory near Jonesboro, Tennessee, in 1796. Bean rifles are so plain that, at first glance, they appear homely and crude. The stock is reinforced by a rectangular piece of metal, and the patch-box, built into the stock, is an elongated wooden door rather than a fancy brass container. It is a "degenerate style" of the original long rifle, as one expert says, but it inspires awe among collectors. Its stripped-down elegance reveals that the beauty of the long rifle is not in ornament but in its lines, the elongated, tapered wand of wood and forged metal that delivers a pellet of lead along the bead of the hunter's sight.

It is an excellent killing machine.

What creates this deadly accuracy and sets a mountain rifle apart from earlier weapons and modern shotguns is a secret hidden inside the barrel, a tiny, spiraling groove etched along the inner surface. In older guns with a smooth bore, the bullet emerged without rotation. Like a knuckleball, it floated dead in the air and was subject to drift, making early pistol duels a relatively safe way of ending a dispute. But the rifle bullet, like a pitcher's fast ball, spins through the air—rips the air, we like to say—with a much better chance of finding its target.

The barrel of a mountain gun is a mixture of will and grace. The outside of it had to be pounded into shape on a battered gun anvil, a hunk of iron gouged with cups and ridges as well as grooves thick enough to hold a gun barrel. In antique stores these anvils are sold as doorstops, a tribute to their primary function, inertia, the anvil holding its shape no matter how much the blacksmith at the bloomery bangs away on it. Over this anvil the outside of the barrel is beaten into submission.

The inside of a rifle barrel is another matter. It has to be teased into shape. The smith puts away his hammer and etches into the metal a groove as delicate as a tendril, a long, thin line that can no longer be forged—or forced. In fact, it cannot even be seen. To set this spiral groove, the gunsmith cuts a line with a rifling guide, a device made from a long strip of wood with grooves running lengthwise along the sides in a long, slow spiral. It looks like an enormous twisted stick of licorice. A dowel with a blade is hooked firmly to one end of this rifling guide and set so that it can pass through the barrel of the gun. As the guide is pulled through a wooden block, it slowly twists, and the knife, running along the inside of the gun barrel, twists too, cutting a perfect rifle groove into the metal.

The guide is a work of art, making external the shape hidden in the gun, but it is the rifled groove itself, glimpsed as a finely etched rosette of lines if we dare look down the long barrel, but otherwise invisible, that seizes the imagination. The ball rides the rifling in the barrel and traces the line on air. The shape of vine and fiddlehead and twisted strands of DNA, the rifled line sets the bullet spinning—whizzing—to its mark, and, like the bit of a drill, through its mark.

According to their songs, mountain folk have an assortment of ways other than guns to kill each other. Silver daggers and the hangman's rope are two. Drowning is common. In one mountain song a man named Johnny Sands, bent apparently on suicide, asks his shrewish wife to bind his hands and push him in a river. She eagerly agrees, but when she runs down the hill to give him a shove, he steps aside and she goes in the water instead, "splashing, dashing like a fish" and crying, "Save me, Johnny Sands." In the last two lines of the song, Johnny regrets that he cannot.

I would my dear for much I wish
But you have tied my hands.

Drowning has its virtues—it leaves no fingerprints or murder weapon behind—and the silver dagger is certainly poetic, but the preferred method for murder in the mountains is to blow the victim away with a gun. "Went out last night to take a little round," the song "Little Sadie" begins. "I met little Sadie and I blowed her down," the next line adds in one of the most compact murder stories ever composed. The brevity, the juxtaposition of a night's stroll with murder, is unnerving, almost comical, so that the killing has a motiveless, even random, feel to it. The murderer—a man named Lee, one version tells us—goes home and sleeps, the ".44 smokeless" under his head, but smoke or no smoke, some plume of regret finds its way into the recesses of the killer's numbed conscience, and the rest of the tale unfolds like a guilt-driven nightmare.

"I began to think what a deed I done," the killer announces when rising the next day, his self-examination coming pitifully after the fact. There is some attempt, muted in this truncated tale, to make Lee a victim. He is apprehended while trying to read his own wanted poster, and asks the sheriff to read the arrest papers to him. He has no money for bail, is paraded through town dressed in black, and is crammed in a county jail cell. He is a killer without a clue, his crime an impulse, his verdict given in words that he cannot read for himself. The judge stands ominously reading from the papers that condemn him. Whether he is a victim or not, though, Lee must pay—that is the code of mountain song. "Forty-one days, forty-one nights," the judge says at the end of the song. "Forty-one years to wear the ball and stripes."

"Little Sadie" is, like most mountain songs, a morality tale, a call for justice in a world of random violence, but hearing it—especially when the song is plunked out on a banjo—I find it hard to muster up much indignation. Pity is the more likely emotion, and, perhaps, puzzlement at human weakness and the amoral life. Innocent, silly, baby-faced boys make guns with their fingers until one day, in anger, in foolishness, or by accident a real gun "goes off," someone bends over a wound, and innocence, empowered, takes its toll. Murder is child's play, the song says, the gun, not the man, doing the killing.

In "Wild Bill Jones," a companion song to "Sadie," a jealous lover shoots Wild Bill dead. "I drew my pistol from my side," the killer says, "and blew away that poor boy's soul," the gun robbing life, and the word *boy* robbing manhood, from the victim. "My age," complains Wild Bill at the beginning of the song,

> is twenty-one.
> Too old for to be controlled.

But age does not matter. When turned on other people, guns are toys, these songs tell us, a symptom in the chaos of our lives of weakness and fear, and we are, by their violence, reduced to children.

When I was a boy, my dad gave me a gun. He unlocked a metal chest and gestured with his arm that I should choose one of the guns lined up before me. My hand went instinctively to the Winchester, a shotgun of an old design that had to be loaded by cocking the barrel and dropping shells into the chamber.

"It's yours," he said, lifting the gun out of the rack and handing it to me. "Use it today."

It was the beauty of wood that caught my eye. Gun stocks—who would disagree with this?—are beautiful. Following the design hidden in the walnut grain, the stock is shaved to conform to the hunter's shoulder in a simple blend of the human and the natural. Old mountain smiths used a drawing knife—a blade held in two hands and brought toward the body—to get the block of wood down to the basic shape they wanted. Chisels, planes, and knives did the rest, the wood sanded and polished until it glowed. If the barrel is a triumph of will, the stock—and the increasingly fussy tools used to shape it—is the opposite: it wears its stripes, the grain that nature gave it, for all the world to see.

Dad and I went skeet hunting that afternoon—I was probably fourteen—and he called "pull" as I held the gun to my shoulder, took careful aim at a clay pigeon in flight, and usually missed, an inauspicious marker along my rite of passage. Later, after I had moved to Georgia and started a family of my own, my Dad and I would meet in Maryland every December to hunt geese, and the Winchester was the gun I used. "It's waiting for you," Dad would say on the morning of the hunt. As we walked together in the predawn light, heading for the blind, our breath a mist on the cold dark air, I would cradle the gun in my arm, and while in the blind, listening for geese honking high overhead, the gun was never far from my hand. It stood—as it stands now in memory—a stiff sentinel and silent witness to filial gratitude. I used it all of the days—the few days—we were able to hunt together. It is, I think, the only gun I have ever fired.

Not long after Dad died, my stepmother took me to the gun rack and told me to choose the ones that I wanted. I knew right away which gun was mine. Dutiful and dismayed, I took it home. On the long drive I thought about cold mornings and a mother-of-pearl sky, and suddenly missed my father very much and was happy for the souvenir. But no sooner did I pull into the driveway of our house than I knew I couldn't keep it. I'm no hunter. I went with Dad to be with him, not to shoot. The gun was useless to me. Also—and this was irreducible—my mother died by a gun, shot herself when I was a boy, and I had promised myself I would never keep one in the house. So I sold it to a friend who was amazed that I would part with a fine piece in such excellent condition, especially one given to me by my father. If I ever changed my mind he would sell it back, he said. My mind, though, was made up.

But—and this is the heart of the matter—I loved the gun. My attachment to it was not just sentimental, not just because it was a gift from my father. It went deeper. Sometimes I waited for hours alone in the gooseblind, sitting still, while I did nothing but listen to geese and watch, with a steady gaze, the checkering on the stock of the gun. I loved the uniformity of crosshatches waffled into the wood and forearm grip, and the way sunlight, filtered through a mesh of camouflaging straw above the blind, puddled on the polished surface like poured syrup. Some say that checkering was the invention of bored hunters who whittled on the stocks of their guns while waiting for squirrel or deer, killing time by making wood beautiful. I would like to think that my response was purely aesthetic, too, unconnected with killing.

But death is built into the attraction of all guns and part of their seduction. It is eerie how easily a gun comes to the hand, as if hands were made for weapons, the fingertips irresistibly drawn to the stock. This attraction—this impulse to take the gun—wears off in time, and after an hour or so of frenzied waiting in a cold blind, the hand may be held to the gun by little more than the warmth it has given away, but when geese appear, honking and bobbing like church bells suspended in air, drawn to their deaths by a lonesome call and handsomely carved decoys, the hunter inevitably stands, brings the checkered stock to his cheek, and, driven by a love he had not known was in him, tightens his grip and pulls the trigger.

In *Guns in American Life,* a critique of America's love affair with guns, Jarvis Anderson examines the "dreadful contradictions" of our love of these killing machines. Words such as *beauty* and *tasteful* are applied to handguns, which have been more "damaging to civilian life" than any other weapon. Gun owners personify the gun with words such as *noble* or *sweet* and give it names like Betsy. The gun may be "a cold machine, a thing of wood and metal," according to Carrol C. Holloway in *Texas Gun Lore,* but "clothed with rich garments of dreams it cannot be cold." The dream, Anderson suggests, takes root early, as guns, and gunslingers, are romanticized on TV and in movies. The Colt .45 commemorating John Wayne came—the ads said—with a "lovely ivory grip" and "elegant packaging," the manufacturers, Anderson writes, inviting buyers to "wrap their hands around the grip of a Colt and imagine themselves 'right back through history.'"

Is that it? These are the myths that no doubt sell guns, the images that those boys carried in their heads, I suppose, as they sauntered out of the pawnshop, one of them wielding a semiautomatic weapon. Is the allure of the gun merely hype, generated by advertisement and pop culture? Or is there something more—something intrinsic to the machine itself?

Part of the allure must be a sense of awe at what guns can do—a sense of all that they can take away and the accompanying feeling of power, a temporary omnipotence. Only those who have never taken a gun in their hands are immune. To resist the urge is, in fact, remarkable. "But you didn't shoot," McCaslin says to Ike in "The Bear" by William Faulkner, and Ike defends the missed opportunity to kill the old foe that he and his family had hunted for years by reading aloud Keats's "Ode on a Grecian Urn" and making an appeal to his cousin. "Courage and honor and pride, and pity and love of justice and liberty," he says. "They all touch the heart, and what the heart holds to becomes the truth, as far as we know truth. Do you see now?" Truth and beauty—it is the Keatsian equation. That is what guns can take away, and, by appropriation, claim.

"Guns in the house are dangerous," my dad said once while locking up the heavy metal footlocker where he stored his rifles. "They fill up a boy's eyes."

My dad loved guns for what they could do—bring a goose out of the sky in a tumbling, flapping, agonized bundle—but his love for them went beyond that. After each day's kill he took the guns apart at the kitchen table under a light—lining up the parts on a towel in the order that he had removed them, cleaning each one. He cleaned the barrel with a cloth—swabbing the inside—and then put all the pieces back together. When he was done—here's the part I remember best—he would hold the gun up in one hand, turning it slightly this way and that in the light, tilting his head, simply admiring it.

It is inevitability that my father loved, gazing down the tube of his weapon, siting some imaginary point in the ceiling above the kitchen window, a feeling akin to the fiddler's string of notes finding its way back to the first chord of a tune. At such moments, Dad's love of what guns do—the reliability of their intricate machinery in the service of the kill—had nothing to do with killing, and, of course, it had everything to do with killing. That is the contradiction, hidden in the gun lover's passions. That is the distancing from blood and lust for blood that makes guns dangerous. The gun has nothing to do with blood, and it puts the bleeding carcass in the hunter's hand.

Inevitability is never pure. It at least has consequences. There may have been no rush of delight in my father when he cleaned his weapons, none of the thrill that he obviously felt when he brought down a mallard on the wing at sixty yards, but his gaze was not idle aesthetic appreciation either. Instead there was a steady beam of love for a machine that did what it—and nothing else—could do, over and over again, superbly. Elegance, not mere beauty, registered on his eye. Sometimes, holding the rifle he had just cleaned at eye level, the light pooling on the polished stock and dying on the charcoal bluing of the barrel, he looked at me and just shook his head, knowing that this kind of appreciation could not be explained. It was something you *got.*

The gun surely empowers, and by its sureness, claims mastery over us as well. Seeing my father there, in memory, holding the gun to the light and turning to his son, I have to smile at the way the image says so much about him and who he was. The analogy—the legacy, I guess—is the image of me lifting a banjo from the towel on my kitchen table after changing the strings, and looking down the neck, eyeing the tension.

When dad slipped the gun into a cloth case for the night and placed it on the rack, he instinctively wiped his hands saying, in so many words, "That's that," as in memory it was, though in life, I know, "that" is never "that"—it leaves a residue, a smudge on our joy. There is a sad song in the offing.

Not long after the smoke had cleared at the assassination of President Garfield, somebody composed a song, the childlike meter and rhyme taking the sting out of the suddenly terrified innocence of Americans. I found the tune on a record by Bascom Lunsford, the banjo player and folklorist from North Carolina. "Going down the street the other day I heard the report of a pistol," Lunsford says, speaking rather than singing the opening lines, as if the ballad emerged out of the reporting of the event. "What does that mean?" At that point Lunsford sings, explaining musically how a president can, in an incomprehensible instant, be killed.

> Oh they tell me Mr. Garfield is shot
> And they're laying mighty low, mighty low.

Though shot, President Garfield is apparently handy to the speaker in our song, who walks up to his bed and asks—what else?—"How's you feelin'?" Garfield, on his deathbed, explains that he plans to eat ham, eggs, bacon, and beans before he dies and spends eternity in heaven, and that he would be glad, as well, for his wife to remarry after he is dead. "Don't ever let a chance go by," Lunsford's tenor voice croons. It's a great moment in folk song. When Garfield dies—full as a tick, I suppose—his wife puts roses on the grave.

In a lawless world, a world where the keeper of laws, the president, can be shot, we have little recourse. The song—the cry for justice—is our only revenge. It keeps our roses red and is where on earth we spend eternity.

The hardest job for the goose hunter is sitting still all day in gray, dank, icy weather. The cold of the air seeps into coats, the cold of the floor seeps into boots, and the cold of the seats seeps into long johns. When I hunted with Dad, we passed time by eating chocolate and sipping coffee, till the coffee got cold, and when all that was done, we pulled in our shoulders and shrank into our coats, savoring what was left of our body heat. Nothing helped. Well, wiggling might have helped, but my father's instructions were emphatic. Don't move. So we sat, sometimes three or four of us, hunkered down in woolens and holding the rifle in front of us silent and still as monks in prayer.

In addition to sudden movement, shiny metal spooks birds, so gun barrels are dulled to a sooty iridescence created by a process called bluing. Almost anything that rusts metal can be used to blue a gun barrel—salt, green walnut hulls, or horse manure mixed with water will work. The trick is not letting the process go too long, since that will pit the surface. Hacker Martin—who was perhaps the best of the modern mountain gunsmiths—described his method of bluing a rifle this way:

> Use a quart of cheap alcohol, to keep her from freezing, and a quart of common cooking water. Rain or soft water is best, of course. Into that throw a handful of bluestone and an ounce or two of nitric acid. Fill up the gallon glass jug with chamber lye from your bed pot. Cork your jug and shake her once in a while so the ingredients will dissolve and mix up good.

Rain, piss, and moonshine age into an *aqua fortis.* Martin, who is a card, writes: "I use it by smearing some on with a common cotton rag on a stick or," he adds, "with your fingers."

Bluing causes metal to absorb light, to trap it, the light running through the blue in broken, geometrical patterns like the lines of light in a star sapphire or the dull glitter of galvanized steel, light playing along the surface, but never escaping. For hours under an achingly cold and mercilessly gray sky I watched what was left of the sunlight disperse along the barrel of the gun, muted and vagrant, the day elongated and in miniature transformed by the phosphorescent glow of the metal to a moonless, midnight scene. Beauty trapped—that's what I watched during hours of numbed contemplation. A blue beauty, glinting and uncontrollable, as slippery as spilt oil and ephemeral as nocturnal flight. Beauty blued, imprisoned, muffled in camouflage and consigned to one task: the kill.

The kill. A bullet has a dull, simple shape with one excuse for being—to penetrate flesh. Mountain smiths made bullet molds with a "cherry," a strip of metal, bobbed at the end, like a note on a stem. Primitive bullet molds were also carved in stone—a base stone with a lid that had holes at the top for pouring the molten lead. The bullet that formed was irregular and crude, but blasting out of the long barrel of the rifle, it was deadly enough to bring home food. Today the bullets come encased in a shell, and the shells can be worn in straps over the shoulder in a frightening array of firepower. There are bullets that cut through metal and, worse, bullets that on impact explode. Boys in a pawnshop can buy them when they tire of pretending to blow people away with their fingertips.

The gun barrel may be elegant and the stock handsome, but the bullet is ugly. Emptiness gathers about its shape. Ridged, ribbed, tapered, or scored with lines, it is meant for travel on thin air. It rides a spark and blast, spinning through the whirligig of the rifle barrel, and emerges whizzing on a single buzzing note, neither rising nor falling for three hundred feet, apparently defying gravity, and before the hunter can blink an eye, finding a target—some home—in tree or dirt, and at times a softer landing in flesh, lodging deep in a puddle of blood.

I have a photograph of two men in overalls, one holding a homemade banjo and the other a percussion rifle. The mountain behind them is stripped of trees, suggesting that the photo is from the thirties, when logging came to the region. The banjo player is clearly proud of his instrument. He stares straight at us, a flat smile across his face, his hand held in the clawhammer position. It is harder to tell about the man with the rifle, because he holds the gun to his cheek, as if to fire, and his hand and the gun stock hide his face, but he also holds a noble pose, and I suspect that the face behind the gun is smiling, too, as proud of his prized possession as the musician. Both the neck of the banjo and the barrel of the rifle point off, toward the side of the photo, in parallel lines.

Guns and song. Near anagrams, the words echo one another.

Before mountain gunsmiths varnish the stocks of their rifles, they often stain the wood with lines of soot to make the polished surface look like the back of a fiddle. When they drill metal parts, they use a bow drill, holding the drill against the chest and moving the bow back and forth, looking just like a country fiddler. Music and weapons have an ancient connection. Trumpets, bagpipes, fifes, and drums have led warriors into battle, and the lyre and the fiddle have offered solace when the killing was done. During the Civil War banjo music could be heard above encampments plunking out sentimental tunes late into the night. Celts, I have read, would declare intermission in battles while minstrels played songs of home, and epics of war—from Homer to Beowulf—set the stories of fighting and agony and valor to music so that the tales rang in the ears of victor and vanquished alike.

I would like to say that music is compensatory, there merely as a comfort, a solace after the violence and the kill. I would like to think of song in opposition to the gun, the music somehow wiping out and replacing the blast and the report of the weapon, but I know that even though music offers some compensation for violence, it is not entirely innocent. The banjo hangs in the same room as the rifle, and the thrill of hitting the fifth string and cocking a pistol are not opposite but akin. Mountain banjo players often talk about "cocking" the fifth string. Alien as music and violence may seem—one bringing agony and the other balm—the machines of death and song have the same source in the inventive and manipulative nature of human beings who cannot refrain from creating objects that express their nature. The banjo and the rifle are the products of the same pair of hands. Taken together, they identify us—smoke and words and lead and song sent out into the world by these buffed and crafted agents of the death and delight that are in us and are us.

Held in the arms, but brought to the eye, the gun answers some need deep in the gut—hunger, yes, when the gun was first invented, but more than hunger. It brings into focus the object of desire, an animal, self-contained in the wild, and with a single report fells it, helpless, as the hunter drops the oiled barrel from his eye and holding the checked stock in his grip, walks to what has now become his, the shot echoing in the hills around him like a song.

Dying in Song

> One died in metaphor and another in song.
>
> —Alexander Pope

The brochure from Georgia Mountain Fair, Inc., arrived without fanfare in my mailbox, and I opened it on the way to teach a class on lyric poetry. "You are invited to take part in our 1997 Official State Fiddlers Convention held in the Anderson Music Hall," the letter said. This is Georgia's "Oldest and Only Convention of Fiddlers." The letter contained "gate admission information" and was signed by one of my heroes, the mountain fiddler Howard Cunningham, who, when he puts down his bow, is the chairman of the Country Music Shows.

According to the "Registration and Course of Events" the contest would last two days. Fiddlers, of course, came first ("15 years & younger") and last ("60 years & over") with a "junior" category for fiddlers under 60 somewhere in between. Fiddlers of all ages were told to play two tunes, one fast and one slow. "Trick or novelty tunes as well as 'Black Mountain Rag,' 'Orange Blossom Special,' and 'Mockin' Bird' are not permitted," the rules admonished fiddlers, "and will be disqualified."

The contest was not just for fiddlers. There was room for harmonica (single reed only), dulcimer, dobro ("not to be confused with bottle neck guitar styles"), bluegrass bands ("No drums! No electric instruments!"), acoustic guitar, five-string banjo, mandolin, and buck dancing (to "No Holds Barred").

I scanned the page while walking—students streaming by me in the hall—and suddenly stopped. Among the other events, there it was. "Old Tyme Banjo." "The old tyme banjo will be interpreted as banjo played in drop-thumb or frailing fashion, not to be confused with 3-finger or bluegrass style banjo playing. Old tyme banjo players will play two (2) numbers of choice." I stood there in the congested hall, one among many, set apart by a mission, the words glowing in my hand. God, in the form of a letter from Howard Cunningham, had called my name.

With John Donne under my arm, I walked into class, carrying a picture—a dream image—in my head. In it I was standing amid a grand chorus: harmonicas tooting, dulcimers jangling, a gaggle of drumless unelectrified bluegrass bands off in the distance, and buck dancers stepping high and all smiles with knees and elbows flaring to "No Holds Barred." And there I was in the midst of the happy throng—gawky and certainly unpoetic—a banjo on my knee. The winner, I read, will take home a trophy and a prize of seventy-five dollars. "That's it!" I announced to dumbfounded students of the Renaissance lyric. "I'm entering the Old Tyme Banjo Contest"—and then, to stifle immediately the accusation that I had wandered off the subject once again, I spelled it for them, "Old Tyme: T-*y*-m-e."

My banjo, I knew, was up to snuff—even if I was not. I had worked an overload at the college in order to earn the money for it. "That's a lot of poetry to invest in a banjo," my wife said. Not only did I have to wade through pages of verse, as well as pages upon pages of comma splices and sentence fragments from student papers, to earn my banjo, I also had to wait out the UPS strike, which I followed in the news as if it were Armageddon.

At last the instrument arrived, and it is a beauty, a 1927 Vega Tu-ba-phone with a newly fashioned, 1997, five-string neck made by a master craftsman. The neck is lovely, with a trefoil inlaid at the first fret of the bonded ebony fretboard, a shaded star at the fifth, and a grand flower-pot inlay in the head. The back of the neck is a rich and glossy mahogany, set off with a fine stripe down the center and an inlaid star at the heel.

It is the pot, though, seventy years older than the neck, that I have come to love. The skin head, held in place by thirty brackets, is nearly twelve inches wide, giving the banjo its plunky sound. Inside the opened back pot, a bell-brass Tu-ba-phone tone ring set in the mahogany rim catapults the plunky notes outward and lets the banjo sing. The pot falls heavily in the lap—more like a weapon than a musical instrument. With it I felt empowered. Filled with hubris, I reckoned the muse would pay dividends—now and in the future—and this contest was merely my first installment. The banjo would do just fine.

I had less confidence in myself. I was allowed to take an accompanist, so I asked my friend Rachel Caviness, who plays bass for many groups at the Georgia Mountain Fairgrounds, to back me up. We practiced in the downstairs den, running all too quickly through my repertoire: "Billy in the Lowground," "Soldier's Joy," "Saint Anne's Reel," "Mississippi Sawyer," and "Whiskey Before Breakfast." I gave it my all. The stroke I use on the banjo goes by various names: clawhammer, drop thumb, thumb cocking, frailing, whamming, rapping, framming, and thumping. I did a little of all of that, dropping thumbs all along the way usually at breakneck speed. When at last I stopped, Rachel looked at me and said, "Is that the best you can do?"

Out of breath, I nodded.

"You'll get blown away."

Rachel probably didn't say that, exactly. She is a sweet southern lady, not given to coarse and clichéd metaphors. But whatever she said, it registered in my ears as "blown away." She told me about last year's contest when the fourteen-year-old "boys from Tennessee," who have each been playing banjo for a hundred years, took all the trophies. "It's great that you're entering, Steve," she said, "but you don't stand a chance."

The banjo has always been an instrument of hope. It was one of the few sources of solace for slaves who brought memories of the mbanza from Africa and built their own banjos from gourds here in America. Unlike the fiddle or the guitar, the banjo came into its own, and achieved its greatest splendor, during the industrial revolution that followed the Civil War. It was a time of innovators, speculators, and entrepreneurs—as well as crooks and cranks—and the banjo, in all of its glitter, represented the age. There is as much metal as wood in the rims of this great generation of banjo innovators: A. C. Fairbanks, William A. Cole, and S. S. Stewart. A Whyte Ladie or Tu-Ba-Phone weighs a ton, lending an industrial authority and confidence to its sound.

The ads for banjos in the late nineteenth and early twentieth century reveal the soul of the newfangled machine. They are filled with the kind of superlatives we associate with traveling medicine shows, words like "choicest," "special," "grand," and "scientifically constructed." Ads boldly announce "new processes" for improved sound, all of them patented, like the medicines of the time. There even was a banjo made with a light bulb in the body offering "indescribable advantages in connection with keeping the Banjo in perfect sounding condition." "Electric," "Eclipse," "Excelsior," "Tu-Ba-Phone," and "Universal Favorite"—these were the kind of names given to the finest banjos, names that exude the good cheer of the times and look ahead with confidence to a bright technological future. If I went into the Georgia Mountain Fair contest foolishly harboring the hope that I would win, I was not to blame. After hours of practice, I felt choicest and grand and electric with indescribable advantages—everybody's universal favorite. The banjo had worn off on me.

The day of the contest, I was a little giddy in the poetry class. The banjo, I told the students when they thought they had gotten me to ramble once again, is never off the subject. It is the perfect metaphor for the aspirations of foolish creatures like us and therefore always appropriate. Maybe it is the syncopated plunk that gets under our skin, I said, professorially. The notes stumble off the player's fingers with each stroke of the hand, but land upright somehow—on their metrical feet, so to speak, ready to go again.

There is poetry in this, I declared. The basic clawhammer strum that says bum-*dit*-ty, bum-*dit*-ty, over and over, falls, when repeated, into a dactylic rhythm. Hammer on or pull off the string with a finger, or better yet, drop that thumb down a notch from the fifth string to the first or second, and a trochaic rhythm takes over—bum-pa-dit-ty, bum-pa-dit-ty, bum-pa-dit-ty. Alternate them, mix or match, and willy-nilly we have created the sprung rhythm of Gerard Manley Hopkins, the banjo ringing with divine madness in its pursuit of God's grandeur.

What about iambic pentameter, you may ask, the stately cadence of Spenser, Shakespeare, and Milton? Iambic pentameter, that was the first heave, I told my students, quoting Ezra Pound himself, and, leaning across the podium, explained *sotto voce* that with the banjo we have left that worn-out meter far behind. After all, who could go back to the plunk-*strum,* plunk-*strum* of the lowly guitar after the banjo has opened new rhythmic possibilities? If the lub-*dub* of the iamb is the rhythm of the heart, I argued, the banjo puts a catch in the stately measure, the rhythm of the heart in love.

By this time, some of the students had lifted their pens and had begun to take notes, furiously. This sounded like stuff that could be on the test. There is more to the banjo than its bare rhythm, I declared, emboldened by their scratching pens, though rhythm, I admitted, is the core. There is nothing mechanical about a banjo tune, just as there is no poetry in a metrically perfect line. The attack on the strings is so important—it is the content of any tune and is nuanced by the poetry in the banjo player's soul. Like the poet, the clawhammer player composes not to the metronome but to the musical phrase. It is there, in the subtle interplay of rhythm and content, sound and sense, that life's mysteries—delivered in word or song—acquire majesty and depth.

Mercifully, the bell rang.

Class dismissed, I announced, letting out a long ribbon of breath. "Hey man," I heard one student mutter to another. "Wasn't *he* on a tear?" I slumped into my seat exhausted. It was three o'clock. In four hours the contest would begin.

The auditorium, a large, domed amphitheater, was nearly full on the night of the contest—more than a thousand people were there, I guess. I walked in and took a seat in the back. The auditorium was dark except for yellow and blue lights cast on the performers. Raymond Fairchild was on stage with a bluegrass group doing a lot of flashy stuff on "Kickin' Mule": fiddling with his Scruggs pegs, playing every fret up the neck, plucking behind the bridge, and for a while picking out the tune on his microphone. The fellow beside me clapped, whistled, stood up, and punched my shoulder, giving me an "Isn't-that-somethin'" wink. It made me sick. Soon I would be up there—out of tune, out of breath, out of my mind, and all thumbs. I thought of looking out over those faces, a wedge of blackness pointing at me. The phrase "blown away" came to mind.

I decided to go backstage. It was crazy there, too, but, after a glimpse of the darkness beyond the curtains, I took comfort in the mayhem. A harmonica player faced a wall, a dulcimer player hid behind a file cabinet, and young fiddlers were everywhere sawing away, creating a happy cacophony. At different times it sounded like a waterfall, a lonesome train, or a pile of rocks rolled into a snake pit—the simile depending on my mood. I went through many similes.

I opened a door to a room normally reserved for the house band, a den with paneled walls, shag carpet, and several low-slung sofas. There were more file cabinets here, a coat rack, and in every corner four or five cases for instruments. I unpacked the banjo and began fiddling with the pegs.

"I'm just tuning," I said when one of the pickers for the house band dropped in.

"Great," he said. "When you're done, tune mine." Then he announced that he had to use the "Bluegrass Bathroom" and left.

Don Sorrell, a banjo contestant, came in next, wearing a formidable-looking banjo hat, a fisherman's cap with tiny banjos instead of lures pinned to it, including one with a pot made out of a walnut. He handed me the hat, pointing to the five threads that were the walnut banjo's strings. "You can almost play that one, it's so lifelike." Don opened his banjo—a handmade, gold-plated beauty—and ran his hand over the strings for a few quick licks. Notes came out of nowhere filling the room with a bold and brassy sound.

"Now that's picking," he said to me with a wink. Suddenly I decided it was time for *me* to use the Bluegrass Bathroom.

When I came back Don Sorrell was gone, but Gwen and Don Oglesby had set up. Gwen was in the dulcimer contest and was running through her piece: "Gray Cat on a Tennessee Farm," an Uncle Dave Macon Song. Her husband, Don—a large man with dark hair and a big smile—played stand-up bass for her, only he was big enough that he played it sitting down, holding the bass in his lap as if it were a guitar. The song was beautiful—Gwen's singing lively and superb—and the bass, strummed guitar fashion, was soothing. At least it got the banjo out of my ear for a while.

Gwen wanted to know which instruments were playing before the dulcimer. "I need to know when to start worrying," she said. So I checked for her. Dulcimers came on after the buck dancers, and banjo followed dulcimer. "You don't have to worry until the buck dancing stops," I told her, "and I'm not going to worry until I see you come off the stage," I added, thinking that a lie might cheer us both up.

Ed Teague, another banjo player, came in next, along with Lawton Dyer, his guitarist, and suddenly the room was full of folks unsnapping cases and tuning up. "I reckon I got last place all sewed up tonight," Ed told us, as he lifted his banjo onto his lap. "Come on, play along," he said to me, and we ran through a lovely slow version of Cumberland Gap. I had never heard it done that way, but I liked it.

Lay down, boys, and take a little nap—
We're all goin' down to Cumberland Gap.

The slow version fits the song.

The only "boy from Tennessee" that I found was Robert Peavy—a man in his forties, tall, thin, with a long, narrow beard. He works in the schools "teaching old-time music to young people." It was, he said, the best of both worlds. He had brought some of his students—a couple of fiddlers and buck dancers—and he was also entered in several categories, himself, including the banjo. "It's for them I come," he said, smiling when two of his students dashed past.

The field of banjo performers at the contest was strong, as far as my ears could tell. It included David Brose, the best banjo player I know. But as I chatted with most of them, I no longer felt intimidated. The event did not feel competitive at all. The contestants were kind and willing to share, exchanging licks and jokes and offering one another tips for handling nervousness. I felt as if I were among friends, all of whom had one weird compulsion: the old-time banjo.

Rachel arrived, and we found a quiet corner to tune and go through our numbers. They sounded good—and I felt confident—until I heard something in the hall that made the banjo string in my heart come undone. One of the contestants—a sixteen-year-old boy from Georgia—was tearing through a tune, and many players backstage had gathered around him. The tune was "Mississippi Sawyer," one of my songs, only it sounded like three banjos playing instead of one.

"Well, listen to that," Rachel said, patting me on the shoulder. "It's not better," she whispered to cheer me up. "Just different."

Yeah, right, I thought, as I tuned my banjo for the fiftieth time.

A woman announced that banjo players were next and should line up. Gwen, the dulcimer player—looking radiant and relieved—left the stage. "Now it's time for *you* to start worrying," she said, patting my shoulder as she brushed past me, all smiles. Don followed, toting the bass under his arm like a viola, smiling too. "Good luck," he said to me with a wink.

My strategy, I decided long before I got on stage, was to act as if I were playing the banjo on my front porch, the faces in the dark crowd nothing more than the trees across the street from where I live. Rachel and I walked out onto the lit platform, and I sat before a bank of microphones. As I had suspected, the audience was hidden in darkness, that wedge of black, but I could feel its attention, its anonymous but looming presence. Suddenly my porch seemed far away and long ago.

A sawyer is a log that floats aimlessly, and dangerously, down a river, so "Mississippi Sawyer" seemed appropriate for my first number. I plinked a G string to be sure it sounded right and dug in, my fingers doing their best under the scrutiny of a thousand pairs of eyes. I played about as well as I ever do, though the tune, riding the rough currents of my nervousness, got a little faster as we went along, despite Rachel's thumping bass and my tapping foot. When I pulled my hand away from the last chord, I was out of breath. Suddenly out of the dark came a burst of applause, and Rachel and I exchanged smiles.

My second song was "Whiskey Before Breakfast," which I recently heard described as a good tune about a bad idea. In fact, the idea was looking better all the time, clearly an option some time before my breakfast, I thought. Most of these banjo tunes come in two parts, A and B, and both parts are repeated three times. Somewhere in part A of the second lap, I missed a string, throwing my timing off a little. The flubbed string was a small mistake—noticeable only as a glitch. I had feared that when I made a mistake I would fall apart in a flurry of errors, but the opposite actually happened. I relaxed at last. With the error, I felt my old self once again, and the crowd receded into darkness. Microphones disappeared, the dome opened on a vault of stars, and I was suddenly transported by my fallibility to my porch and the woods beside my house, the song at my fingertips smooth as bourbon, nothing but hardwoods and pines anywhere in earshot.

"How did you do?" Don Sorrell asked when I walked backstage, polite applause ringing in my ears, Rachel saying that I had done fine, as she always does.

"I got about half the notes right," I told Don. "Do you think that's enough?"

I quickly put up my banjo and went to the other side of the stage, where the sound equipment and the technicians were. I wanted to see David

Brose play, and this was the best spot. David, wearing his vest and jacket as usual, set his two banjos in front of him, one that he had borrowed from a friend and the other a "Little Wonder," an antique frailer made by Vega. His first song, which he played and sang, was "Fly Around My Betty," a variation on "Shady Grove" that David picked up in North Carolina. He settled the mikes, told a joke, and started in. No one I know attacks the strings the way David does. His hand, set in a stiff claw, sweeps them without apparent movement at all, sounding four to seven notes as if by magic, each a little bell. They ring delicate and precise but—and this is the trick—never lose the backbeat of an authentic mountain sound. He sang in a reedy baritone, his voice rubbing up against the clatter his hands had raised. I loved hearing his voice, a continuous and modulated sound played against the counterpointed plink of the banjo. Singing was not allowed and probably cost David the contest. A small price to pay, I thought.

The second song, "Napoleon's Crossing," was, David said, "as old as God's dog." He switched banjos, quickly checked the tuning, and started to play, no voice this time, just the banjo. I marveled at how smooth his playing was, notes coming effortlessly out of a thumb-cocked claw that never came unclenched. Nothing forced or flashy—just *right.* He looked relaxed, perfectly at home in front of the crowd, even though he was doing complicated work up the neck. His banjo glittered in the spotlights. Maybe he, too, had found his way to the front porch, the notes rising in the dusky dark dome and setting the stars ablaze, the "Little Wonder" living up to its name.

We had time to kill while the judges deliberated. For a while I talked to David, who warned me not to take a contest too seriously. He told me about the time that he had lost a contest to a woman who had only been playing the banjo for two weeks. The judge was an old banjo player positioned at a table just below the front of the stage. It was the sixties, and the woman wore a miniskirt "cut right to here"—David motioned with his hand at his thigh. "I knew I was sunk," David said, "when the judge's table began to rise."

I spent the rest of the time wiping down my banjo and putting it away. For a while before closing the case I just looked at the instrument. I was tired, a little cranky, and pretty sick of banjos by this time, but the sight of it wrapped in the fuzz lining of its case cheered me up. It was lovely still, the leaves and stems of the flowerpot inlay at its head flickering different colors in the fluorescent light of the Bluegrass Bathroom across the way. The banjo is such a goofy and cantankerous combination of wood, steel, and skin, that it can, in moments like this, remind us of ourselves at our worst, and make us laugh.

Unfortunately, a little banjo is a dangerous thing. Looking at mine so lovely there, I forgot about David, Don, Robert, Ed, and all the others in the running. I also forgot about the truth and entertained a foolish thought. Maybe I'll *place.*

I came in dead last. Rachel, as usual, consoled me. "The points were close," she said, "and you did better than players in other categories." You lost, but you didn't get blown away, she was saying in so many words. Don Sorrell was declared the best banjo player in Georgia. Someone who breezed in for his performance and breezed out without talking to anybody backstage came in second. Robert Peavy from Tennessee was third but seemed to take more delight in his students, all of whom placed. One girl, who came in first in the fiddle contest, waved her prize in the air and declared, "I'm going shopping!"

What struck me when I got home that night and finally did have that whiskey well before breakfast is that I had harbored a hope until the very end that I would win. It is not in my nature to be competitive. At my son's soccer matches I cringe when the parents of his teammates shout at the referee, and I love music because, like poetry, it is not a contest. After all, can anyone really lose in song? Most of the time I play alone on a porch, where music is a matter between a solitary soul and a tolerant God, with all others driven out of earshot.

It was late—the rest of the family had gone to bed—so I went out on the porch. I set the banjo in its place against the porch rail and gave it a toast. Looking at the funny inlays in the neck, the shiny metal hoop, and the silly drum, I saw myself. "I need more plunk in my strike." That was one thought I had, immediately contradicted by the next. "I need to get it smooth." Amorphous ambitions began to take shape in my mind. I devised impossible schemes with hours of the day set aside for banjo practice. I saw myself on stage, but this time perfect, plunky *and* smooth. Maybe next year, I thought, the banjo's irrepressible optimism wearing off on me again, though I felt certain I would never get on that stage again. I plucked a single string, and the note, pure as poetry, rose into the woods, dying on the night sky with no one there but me to hear.

The Aeolian Mode

Why four seasons? Our poets have always known that there are more. "Midwinter spring is," T. S. Eliot writes, "its own season." Perhaps like the days of the week or the ages of man or the dwarfs of legend, there are seven seasons in all, one for each of the ancient musical modes, seasons of transition, seasons of flux. I'm thinking now of those afternoons in early fall, when the day is still warm enough for touch football in shirtsleeves, but as the sun goes down the temperature drops quickly, and a wind, harbinger of cold nights, starts grumbling somewhere in the hollows and gathers momentum, whipping around hills and setting the trees dancing.

In the Dorian mode we hear nothing in the wind, but when we tune up to the Aeolian, we stop and listen and know what we are listening for. By now we have suffered.

The poet Shelley wrote about clouds and wind and air. He and the other Romantics were much taken by aeolian harps, lutes hung in windows and on porches, equipped with a sounding board and a set of strings that vibrate in response to air currents. Coleridge associated the aeolian harp with receptivity in love, the instrument

> *by the desultory breeze caressed,*
> *Like some coy maid half yielding to her lover*

and wondered "if all of animated nature" were "but organic Harps diversely framed." It is a lovely thought that the universe is God's instrument, left on the windowsill of heaven to play our sad and lovely songs. "Make me thy lyre," Shelley wrote, "even as the forest is."

Part of the allure of the word dulcimer *must be its doleful sound—the long* u, *the* mer *at the end. Starting at the teeth and working its way back into our throat, the name is all softness at the edges, all* murmur *and* mere *and* ur. *Dulcimer. It is a sweet girl with a sad look on her face. When it sheds its Dorian irony, it can plumb the depths of woe.*

When I first moved to the mountains more than twenty years ago I lived with my young family at the base of Brasstown Bald, the tallest mountain in Georgia. It was a peaceful spot, with only one house above us and above that a clear stretch of trees to the mountain summit. The trees and the lay of the land hid the mountaintop from us, and most of the time I went my way blithely unaware of the looming presence behind us.

But on stormy nights Brasstown Bald declared itself; the winds, engendered by moiling clouds and riding a nap of whipped and jostled treetops down the mountainside, came roaring by my house. I would walk down to the end of my driveway to roll up car windows or secure trashcan lids and hear, above me, an avalanche of sound, the wind in the Appalachians. No figures of speech can convey the way the world is transformed by wind, though wind is the metaphor of our darkening moods—a breeze of joy, a squall of confusion, and a howling gale for all our woes (woes abstracted, woes distilled) and on these darkened, rain-spitting evenings as I stood at the end of my drive, trashcan lid in hand, that is what I heard, in one long and harmonious drone, all our woe. A change is coming, these fall gusts announce, a modal shift, leaving the Dorian one note behind and far, far away.

One source of these modal variations may be the pentatonic scale—the simple, five-note range of many mountain songs. Since most of the variations in the mode occur at the sixth and seventh notes in the scale, the differences in modes are often disguised. The Aeolian and Dorian are identical through the first five notes, and mountain songs played in one can be transposed to the other with ease. The differences are there but implied, hidden in ambiguity and overtones. The variation is in the absence, in the remainder, and haunts, rather than directs, the song. When the sixth note is sounded—often as a harmony—it can catch us by surprise, like the first winter wind.

In the Aeolian mode we bring in the lawn chairs and hang them from nails in the basement, put up beans, freeze corn, and lock down windows. Knowing that we cannot do everything, we make lists, two-thirds canceled, which lie curled on bureau tops and refrigerator doors. We fill the calendar with the footnotes of our days. We stack firewood and fill bins, ready to wait out the winter. We get restless.

In the Aeolian mode we abandon old loves, aching for something new—or we are abandoned by them. Either way, we acquire a measure of loneliness.

Once I had a dear companion
Indeed I thought he was my love,

one Aeolian song, called "Lonesome Companion," begins.

Until some black-eyed girl betrayed me.
Now he cares no more for me.

All that you love you lose, that is the Aeolian lesson. "Just go and leave me if you wish to," the lonesome girl sings, "that will never bother me," but the plaintive melody and the character of the notes along this scale betray her. Despite her pluck, they say agony. The song ends:

Last night you were so softly sleeping
Dreaming in some soft repose,
While I a poor girl brokenhearted
Listened to the wind that blows.

In the Dorian mode they retreat to separate corners of the house. Separate sides of the bed. In the Aeolian mode, one side is empty.

The Northern Sea

"There lived an old lord by the Northern Sea," I sang absentmindedly, as I played random notes on the black keys of the piano. "By the Northern . . ." I repeated in a whisper and stopped, the piano notes resonating through the empty house, and in the recesses of my mind some mossy stone rolled away, revealing a green headland overlooking the sea. I saw rocks and waves and a spumy salt spray on cliffs below, and above nothing but water and air, the whole scene suddenly visible to me, though I never left the room and my finger still pressed the black piano key. I was in the Georgia mountains at the southern tip of the Appalachians, but the landscape I saw in my mind was England.

Five months later I was in a Fiat heading north on M1, the superhighway that cuts through the heart of England. After staying awake all night watching James Bond on the plane, the merciless sun rising on me six hours too early, I found myself, haggard with jet lag, nosing into three lanes of traffic all, my instincts told me, going the wrong way. When I tried to turn or pass or downshift or click on the radio for that matter, lifelong habits betrayed me. Everything on the English roads felt backward, and, after a half hour of driving, I looked like a bug-eyed lunatic with one obsessive desire: to stop.

Fortunately my teenage daughter, Nessa, was with me, a map on her lap and a smile on her face, chipper and excited. Sitting on the right side of the car, I had a tendency—I don't know why—to hug the left side of my lane so Nessa dug deep fingerprints into the upholstery on her door, cars whizzing by mere inches away from her ear. She whimpered some but generally was a good sport about these brushes with death.

Eventually we turned off of the M1, and some of the traffic began to clear. On a quieter stretch of road, Nessa, reluctantly leaving the driving to me, slept. "I know where I'm going," my wife would sing years ago when Nessa was a baby, reaching behind me, rocking the car seat, as I drove the station wagon at night through mountains on the way home. "And I know who's going with me." Where *was* I going, I wondered now, risking a glance away from the English highway to see my girl—a young woman—curled up beside me, her coat for a pillow?

We had an itinerary for points north—Scarborough, Whitby—and we had plans, too, the addresses of bed and breakfast spots picked out all along the way. Ahead was a castle, an inn, and a seacoast, and I knew the names of much that I would find there. But I knew—as sure as the sight of my college girl asleep brought back thoughts of her as a baby—that I was not headed forward at all, but back, back in time, to a place that does not exist except as it is lodged in song.

No one knows how—or where—our songs began. One poet, speculating on the origins of his craft, believes that poetry and song, the sounds we make with our voices, are born out of the imitative urge. "Crouched by the fire near the cave mouth and listening to thunder reverberating among the rocks," John Frederick Nims writes, early humans "must have amused or frightened themselves by making thunder-sounds deep in the throat—probably bursting into wild, delighted laughter at their success or lack of it." Like poetry, songs appear when humans appear, and as Indo-European tribes migrated out of the Caucasus, they must have brought the thunder and crack and rain of their words and songs with them into the northern reaches of the European continent.

Folk music came across the Northern Sea to the coast of England on the lips of Anglo-Saxon warriors in the fifth century. Eventually the songs spread everywhere in the British Isles, though the stronghold for singing remained the point of entry, the northern borderlands where the Angles had first settled, the "north countreye" of so many ballads. This is where Nessa and I were headed—to the moors and seacoasts of northern England, far removed from the southern metropolises. We headed for the beginnings of song in our language.

Scarborough is an ancient English port associated with the folk song called the "Elfin Knight," familiar to most of us as "Scarborough Fair." The ruins of the castle at Scarborough stand in a promontory of land jutting into the sea. Steep cliffs and a large, grassy headland make a perfect natural fortress, and the keep itself—the largest part of the castle remains—has a commanding view of both the northern and southern harbors of the town and, of course, the wide horizon of the sea itself. The area was originally settled by Vikings—the town named for a Viking king—and later was occupied by Romans and Normans. John Wesley preached here—seventeen times, a marker in town says. This is Brontë country, too—Anne is buried at Saint Mary's in town, and the Yorkshire moors, made famous in Brontë novels, loom as a presence just beyond the edge of town.

The harbor overlooking the North Sea is particularly beautiful. Storms blew in the day I arrived, waves in tiers crashing on the shoreline. The narrow shore butts against a cliff forty or fifty feet high. Cars roar and honk by day along the road that winds its way at the cliff edge. At night, street lamps illuminate the coast, a lit path following the line of cliffs off to the moors. It was the place I had seen in my mind while sounding keys on the piano in my living room. Now, standing at the cliff's edge, I heard the sea and wind moan.

The "Elfin Knight," created out of an incongruous mix of farm and sea imagery, is a contest song between lovers who set impossible tasks for each other. In it a woman must make "a cambrick shirt" that shows "no seam or needle work." If she will do that and wash it in a dry well and dry it on a thorn "which never bore blossom since Adam was born"—well, if she will do all these things then the man will consent to be her true love. Not to be outdone, the woman agrees, but only, according to several versions of the song, on the condition that the man will farm the beach, sowing it with a single peppercorn, harvesting it with a "strap o leather," and stacking the harvest in—of all places—the sea, tying up the works with a peacock's feather. When you are finished, the woman adds coyly, you can come pick up your cambric shirt.

Standing here, at the ridge by Scarborough, I see the strand stretching unfarmed for miles and thorn bushes unadorned. My shirt, hidden under my wool coat, shows—I know without looking—seams. Most of all, I see how high I am above sea level, lifted by this windy headland to a spot with a nearly endless view of what is far away and beyond my grasp. Here I, too, am tempted to ask for more than life can give. "Ance she was a true love of mine," goes a Scottish version of the refrain, the line, the burden, carrying the agony of this otherwise playful ballad. "The Elfin Knight" is about lovers sowing the sand and a shirt that no one will wear.

I made the rounds of the pubs in Scarborough in the hope of hearing music—I visited many of them, believe me—but I never heard a song except for recordings played over speakers. I didn't want to go to a festival. I wanted to hear the songs that people really sang, but when I asked about live music, the folks at one bar laughed and said that my best bet was an Elvis impersonator. "He really is very funny," the bartender said with a wink. At the same bar I met a professional karaoke singer—I didn't know that there were such people. He loved Americans and did impersonations of Barry Manilow.

His name was Joe, and he was from north of Scarborough, a Northumber the others called him derisively, making fun of his accent and insistent, demonstrative manner. "We think folks from up North are a little cracked," one of the men at the bar said. But coming from the mountains north of Atlanta—a part of Appalachia that is still the butt of many jokes—I was sympathetic to Joe. "There is scarce an old historical song or ballad whereon a minstrel or harper appears, but he is characterized by way of eminence to have been 'of the North countreye,'" wrote Thomas Percy in the *Reliques of Ancient Poetry,* published in 1765, adding that "the prevalence of the northern dialect in such compositions shows that the representation is real." Northern England, not unlike the mountains where I live, is distant from cities like London and Liverpool, and, as Percy points out, its people "would preserve their ancient manners longest," so it seemed sad that Joe—a wandering singer—made his living by performing Barry Manilow impersonations at a seaside resort.

And yet, it has always been that way, hasn't it? In the time of Queen Elizabeth, a typical court musician, Percy explains, wore the robes of nobility, combed his hair "with a sponge daintily dipt in a little capon's grease . . . to make it chine like a Mallard's wing," wore a shirt after "the new trink," a long cape "of Kendall green" gathered at the neck with a "narrow gorget," and "ruff fair starched" so that each "stood up like a wafer." At the same time, beyond the walls of court, minstrels roamed the countryside "wandering abroad" in such a wretched state they could not—as an edict of the queen stated—be distinguished from "rogues, vagabonds, and sturdy beggars."

Isn't the art of folk music always in disguise? Isn't it always wearing the trappings of its listeners? Isn't it played on whatever instrument comes to hand? Even a karaoke?

There is no single town where we can say the English folk song started. It spread as soon as it arrived. But when I trace the English ballad back to its source, I'm driven to some town like Scarborough with a ruined castle, a rocky harbor, ravens in the air, and a wide North Sea horizon. The folk songs that eventually made their way to the hollows of the Appalachian Mountains entered our language through ancient ports like these, ports known for fishing and smuggling and, of course, singing.

But coasts are either beginnings or ends—the turbulent places where adventures start or come crashing to a conclusion—and Scarborough, after several days of wandering its narrow streets, began to feel to me like an ending. The rocks say so, located in black heaps where the breakers crash. The ruin of the castle, hoary and grim, built of the same stone as the land itself, has an air of finality about it, too. Even the moorish landscape of hedges and soft grass say return, say soft landings, say home at last.

The north harbor of Scarborough braces itself each winter for strong winds and heavy seas, and the keeper of the rooms where Nessa and I stayed said that in gales the water, buttressed by winds, rises up the sea wall and the cliffs and crashes against cars and houses there. As I threw our bags into the car, I stopped to look at the sea—the day windy, the water churned gray—and thought of the dream I had had of this place while randomly playing the keys on the piano thousands of miles away. Standing here, I heard no music. In its place was the inhuman roar of the waves, a source and gravestone of my songs. As Nessa and I drove off, heading south along the strand, hugging the curve, the waves crashed against the sea wall in farewell, a spume of salt water rising house high and descending on the hood of the car in a mist.

We arrived from the "north countreye" intact, somehow, though we drove through a London suburb searching desperately for the car rental building, took a train and a subway into downtown London in the middle of the night carrying luggage, got off at the wrong station downtown (Euston Square rather than Euston), flagged a taxi that threw a belt, and arrived bedraggled in a hotel staffed by émigrés from the Continent who spoke impeccable English and sneered impeccably as well.

The next morning the world looked brighter. Our hosts were charming and helpful with directions, and we headed for the British Museum. Once there, Nessa struck out on her own to find the Rosetta Stone and other treasures. I had come to see ancient medieval songbooks and—waiting for permission to enter the manuscript room—began by just wandering around. Galleries were filled with furniture, clothing, jewelry, and utensils from others eras, even a room set aside for clocks, but "no instruments, I'm afraid," said a woman in a blue coat at the information desk, and just when I was about to give up, I wandered into the room dedicated to the artifacts recovered at Sutton Hoo and saw the harp—a reconstructed version—hanging above the display of original fragments.

The fragments are parts of an ancient lyre, bits of gilt bronze escutcheons and maple wood that had been wedged for more than fourteen hundred years between bronze pots in the remains of the grave ship of a fifth-century Anglo-Saxon king. Only the yoke and arms of the lyre, marked with holes that once held willow pegs, survive, attached at the joints by bronze tacks. The rest of the instrument, hollowed out for resonance, is rotted and gone. Parts of the bridge, carved in amber, remain. An eighth-century manuscript illustration of King David playing a lyre, reproduced from the Cotton Vespasian manuscript—shows that this kind of ancient lyre was plucked or strummed by the right hand and fingered, through the opening in the lyre's arms, at the back—a string for each finger, with one open string for the drone.

But it is the escutcheons that catch the eye, elaborately shaped bronze circles with knotted designs molded into them, medallions of something ancient and remote, calling us back to our oldest songs, to a time when ancient Angle kings would hear the harpist and drink from vessels made of long, twisting auroch's horns while gaming with ivory dice, the music mixing with laughter and shouting and tears.

The poem *Beowulf,* a product of the culture that produced the artifacts found at Sutton Hoo, opens with the funeral of Skyld, the folk king of the Danes, whose body is laid out "in the waist of the ship" with a "mound of treasures from far countries." The hold was freighted with "weapons of a warrior, war accoutrements, swords and body armour," and on his chest "were set treasures and trappings to travel with him on his far faring into the flood's sway." Above his head they "hoisted and fixed a gold signeur." When the preparations were completed, they "gave him to the flood," uncertain who "unshipped that cargo." From the archeological discovery at Sutton Hoo, we know that one object in with the knives and helmet and swords and shield in the king's ship was a harp. These violent men carried a song in their hearts.

In the banquet scene in the middle of *Beowulf,* the gleeman takes down his harp to perform the "Lay of Finn," a ballad about a king who makes a compromise with his enemies and dies for his treachery. The men at the banquet are about to go to war, many to their doom. "String and song sounded together," "gladness mounted," and "bench-mirth rang out" as women poured wine, the men, for the moment, feeling a kinship created by the song. Their "bond was sound at that time," and "each was true to the other." Many will die, but for now, in a space carved out by a harp and a voice, they are spared "the weird they did not know destined from old."

After an hour or so I was allowed to leave the commotion of the museum's exhibit halls behind and enter the silence of the rare manuscript room. There, among scholars, I took a seat at a desk in front of a wooden podium with a sheet of Plexiglas set ominously beside it. The Plexiglas, I realized, was for holding down the pages so that I could read a book without touching it. I undid my notes and waited, pencil in hand—pens are forbidden—and watched the clock. A half hour later an attendant placed the Sloane manuscript beside me.

Sloane is dated 1450, making it one of the oldest written sources of English songs. The cover, a mottled red and brown, was obviously added by the museum. On the front and back it bears the Latin inscription BIBLIOTECA MANUSCRIPT SLOANEIANA. The book's spine has a subtitle, OLD ENGLISH POEMS with SLOANE embossed at the bottom. The pages are small, no more than five inches high, and gray, with a brown color showing through the vellum, and so old that they are nearly translucent. Torn at the bottom, the pages are pitted and rounded at the edges. The ink is light brown, too, as many as twenty-six lines of tiny script crammed on a page slightly bigger than my hand.

Not only are religious songs here, tunes such as "Saint Stephen and Herod," but secular ones as well, including riddles and folk songs. The book is, in fact, jolly, once we get past the paper's darkening patina. Margins are embellished with trefoils and flowers, some for ornament and some as significant markers, all done with a sure hand: "Lullay lullay lytil chyld" appears on one decorated page, the words among the doodles a toy for the new mother's tongue.

Although the cover identifies the manuscript as a book of poems, it is in fact a songbook, clearly intended for use, with stanzas and refrains marked by dotted lines and symbols. In the British Museum it is kept with care, housed in an air-conditioned vault, the pages turned with a sheet of paper, not the fingers, and much of its battered look undoubtedly came about long before it was housed here. It had, in short, been much loved and much used. In the museum it is a thing for the mind, but before it made its way to this silent room, it was a starting point for the tongue and voice as the lines ending in doodles suggest, words—willy-nilly—turned into music. Best of all, the manuscript ends in unused pages, a few of them scribbled over, hastily, but most blank for five hundred years, waiting an eternity for another song.

The silence in the reading room of the British museum was so thick that when I shut the Sloane manuscript with a soft thud, three heads looked up. There is no music in *this* place, I thought, handing the book to a bored attendant.

Cecil Sharp, the musicologist who fathered the modern English folk revival in the first decade of the twentieth century, knew that the old songs were fragile and under the threat of extinction. He also knew they could not be kept alive in a museum. Folksinging, Sharp argued in 1907, is a "great tradition that stretches back into the mists of the past in one long, unbroken chain, of which the last link is now, alas, being formed." Popular music—in particular the "composed song"—was, he feared, destroying the songs that had grown more naturally from the people themselves. Comparing the folk song to wildflowers, Sharp argued that the English endangered its other cultural accomplishments by ignoring homegrown music. "A country that is too arid to grow wildflowers will scarcely win renown for the beauty of its gardens."

In an attempt to save the old songs he, accompanied at times by his friend the composer Ralph Vaughn Williams, traveled the English countryside—in particular the area of Somerset—gathering some fifteen hundred tunes. As the project grew, so did his ambitions for it, "desultory" collecting giving way to deliberate plans for the "re-introduction of folk songs into our national life." The arena for this project was not the museums but the schools. The songs, he believed, would be best preserved on the voices of English girls and boys.

Not every song would do, though. Folk songs differ from other songs "not in degree but in kind," Sharp wrote. Unlike popular songs—or, for that matter, many broadside ballads created by individuals, true folk songs are a "communal and racial product," which gives them a "national character" and a "fitness to serve a national purpose." Part of his job was to create a collection of acceptable songs to be taught to English schoolchildren.

Sharp's project was enormously successful—it became the method for teaching music in English schools and was the model for countries around the world. Unfortunately, Sharp's attempt to revive folk traditions has little of the whimsy and indigenous spirit necessary for the natural evolution of song, and his program for protecting folk traditions had the effect of embalming them. The true music of the people, lodged in their corrupted hearts, will not be arrested and cannot be frozen. The soul of the song is not in its source, but in the chameleon spirit that lets it change. The oldest folk songs—the most authentic and durable—are not in museums, to be sure, but they are also not in lesson books. They are in the hearts and on the lips of ordinary folk who would never think of putting the word *proper* in front of them.

A friend of mine who teaches music theory tells me that children—when they first learn to sing—progressively acquire notes along the pentatonic scale. When children sing to themselves—or play games like hide-and-seek—the singsong, two-note tune is made up of the fifth and third notes on the scale—*sol* and *mi.* Later, they add the sixth, *la*—all three notes part of the pentatonic. Most nursery rhymes, many hymns, and some ritualistic tunes are pentatonic. "Reveille," for instance, which has jolted generations of recruits out of bed, follows this ancient scale, and "taps"—the soldier's lullaby—is the tune I use to check the pentatonic tuning of my banjo.

Cecil Sharp believed that the pentatonic scale was the litmus test—the dead giveaway—of the authentic folk tune. He notes in his commentary on folk song at the turn of the century that there are few true pentatonic songs left in England—most had been embellished—but in Scotland and the southern Appalachian Mountains of America "the pentatonic scale is common." Dismissing the theory that the Americans took their songs directly from the Scottish, Sharp theorized that the American songs are simply older—purer—versions of the British tunes protected from change in an undeveloped part of the world. "The pentatonic was an earlier form of the scale," he concludes, and "it had been in common use among English peasantry at the time that the ancestors of mountain people left the country."

If Sharp is right, I didn't have to travel to English pubs to hear the songs in the green headland of my imagination. The oldest songs in English may in fact be found in my valley at home, songs that are older than any version I could find in English countryside or coastal towns, songs surviving like a faded photograph on a five-tone scale. The pentatonic does not deliver me to the coast of the Northern Sea or the wreckage at Sutton Hoo or the manuscripts in the British Museum. If it did, it would simply be another gravestone along the way. No, the notes of the black keys on my piano that sent me on this journey took me far away in order to bring me home.

Folk music is music that simply happens. Like life, like disease, it evolves, changing over time, and it is at that unstable point at the edge of change that it parts ways with classical music set on paper and popular music cast in vinyl. It is also at that point that it parts ways with any attempt to authenticate, codify, or—alas—protect it. It lives on in the next voice that sings it and, in doing so, changes it. Folk music cannot be corrupted any more than genes can be corrupted, because its beauty, like human beauty, is what runs through us as we follow our hearts to whatever and whoever happens next.

Recordings freeze a song into a single version for a time, and have an effect on music not unlike that of rule-bound traditionalists such as Cecil Sharp. But the loss is not permanent, a fact often forgotten by the purist. Any popular song, any classical tune, can, in a heartbeat, be returned to the folk tradition, as soon as it leaves the page or the plastic that sets it and holds it and keeps it pretty and dead like a doll, and finds new life in the mouth of someone who by obstinacy, will, poor taste, or lack of talent refuses to do it right—a prince charming in the shower or on some lonely street corner, kissing the song back to life.

The closest I came in England to hearing true folk music was an event in the London underground that happened by chance. A young woman, maybe twenty, wearing a brown vest and dirty blue jeans, her short hair done up wildly in a scarf, banged away on a nylon-string guitar decorated with flowers drawn in colored inks and sang in a powerful contralto voice an old rock-and-roll song by the Seekers called "She's Not There."

It was an impromptu—maybe illegal—performance. There had been some tie-up in one of the stations and the passengers were in rows all along the transom waiting to board delayed trains. The young woman with black hair shoved her way into a corner by a busy section—put a blue plastic bowl at her feet—and began to play for this trapped audience. She strummed full chords with open strings and sang in a loud, harsh voice that carried throughout the station, her words about love and apology and absence echoing through the cavernous halls of the station.

Most commuters, late for appointments and evening concerts and West End musicals, rushed by without acknowledging her. A few threw money in her cup and hurried on. Her quilted vest was trimmed in braid and decorated with paisley in motley and earthy tones, while lacy and gauzy scarves poked out here and there at her cuff and collar and in her hair. Listening to her gravelly voice and watching her anxious eyes, I thought of the minstrels in other centuries who played their music and ran. I knew that Cecil Sharp would not have approved, but saw the flowers on her scarf, in her hair, and penned on her pockets and her guitar. "A country that is too arid to grow wildflowers," I thought, remembering Sharp's own words, "will scarcely win renown for the beauty of its gardens."

The Oldest Answer

I used to live in a house at the base of Brasstown Bald, the tallest mountain in Georgia, where quiet evenings were backed up against a mighty and looming presence. When I walked to the end of our gravel driveway, I often heard the first stirrings of wind along the ridges, a distant tumult of treetops arriving to me as a whisper, a harbinger of storms that come wailing out of nowhere through our valley. An eerie and inhuman call, this wind is the keening of our solitude and a reminder of our loneliness in the world. Standing there with gravel underfoot, my family off in the yellow-lit house, I often felt an ancient longing, the urge to set a voice to the night wind. Here, I thought, is where ballads are born.

"One night," my friend the poet Bettie Sellers told me, "I went just about to the ceiling." She was at her house on another ridge in the shadows of Brasstown Bald when the scream of a mountain lion shattered the quiet. Mountain lions are rare in our region, most of them driven out by fearful mountain residents, and some neighbors who heard Bettie's tale didn't believe her. "I don't care what anybody says," she told me one morning, pointing her finger and squinting with one eye, "it was a mountain lion out behind our house." Relaxing in her seat, she slapped her knee and laughed. "It was the most *eerie* sound." For Bettie it was not just the call of the beast in the woods that was frightening, but the silence that it broke. "When you live where it is *so* quiet," she said, nodding toward the door, "sounds are enough to give you the shivers."

Night sounds do not come from friend or foe; they come from nowhere, a place alien to us, a line drawn on the wind. Bettie describes this silence as the "unexplained," and it has become her calling. "My bent," she said, "was to espouse the unseen that's in the woods at night." That is the urge, felt by those who lived at the base of a howling mountain long before Bettie and I arrived. It is the need to fill all this haunted otherness with something human: a story, perhaps, or a song or a poem. The ballad, of course, is all three at once.

Bettie Sellers, the poet laureate of Georgia, has written ballads herself and has devoted much of her attention to the work of Byron Herbert Reece, the mountain poet from our area who was the finest writer of the literary ballad in our time. Early morning light poured in through glass doors of her place on the hill beyond Corn Creek while she read aloud for me Reece's "Ballad of the Rider," the tale of a man who, knife in hand, is willing to ride his horse into hell to avenge a lover who has left him. Bettie paused at the last stanza.

> And what pale palfrey shall he ride,
> What magic metalled knife
> Have power to harm his wandered bride
> Beyond the leaves of life.

"That use of 'pale palfrey' here," Bettie said, "strikes me interestingly."

Bettie believes that the archaic language in ballads is a throwback to England, an attempt to give the ballads the old-world grandeur their tragedies deserve. "Well, we don't have kings and palaces and pale palfreys here," but the language, "a remnant of European elements," serves a purpose, rendering the text otherworldly. Archaisms are conjuring tools, magic words from a world long ago and far away, taking on the power of incantation and creating a presence in a landscape that otherwise won't have us.

When Bettie reads "The Rider," her voice has the authority of incantation. She cracks her consonants sharply and lingers over vowels, getting all the meat out of words. Coffee smells are drifting about us in the sunlit living room. It is morning. But as Bettie reads aloud, the room seems to darken.

Under the little leaves of life
Helmer rode in a stranger's land
Bearing beneath his coat a knife
Well fitted to his hand.

Like magic formulas, ballads conjure ghostly presences by doubling, by repetition and rhyme. "It's an oral tradition," Bettie explained. "It's only going to be heard once. So main themes are repeated to remind this audience of what is important." The wife in "The Rider" is an intoxicating mixture of joy and seduction. She is his treasure.

Her laugh is free, her step is light,
Her eyes outflamed the dawn,
Her lips were wine of strange delight.

The repetition of these lines throughout the song reminds the listener of what is at stake. It is the horseman's burden—and, for the length of the tune, ours, too—hauled about in haunting reiterations, filling the void with our obsessions. It is, Bettie says, "what we are not allowed to forget."

My favorite ballad is "The Wife of Usher's Well." It is one of the ancient Child ballads, and Reece's mother used to sing a version of it, called "Three Little Babes," to Reece when he was a boy. The first time I heard it I was driving to town on an errand listening to a tape by Hedy West, the banjo player from Carrollton in western Georgia. I was so excited that I had to pull off the road. The banjo, set to a modal G, is plaintive and lovely, the opening melody haunting. "There was a woman," the song begins, and West's voice—part creek, part mountain lion—rides up the pentatonic scale of the opening phrase, lingers on the word "woman," and comes back down the scale for the rest of the line: "and she lived alone."

The mother has sent her children away, to "the north country." The lyrics, and West's singing of them, are soulful and heartfelt, but not solemn at all, the banjo keeping a syncopated, playful rhythm throughout and ending the second line of each stanza with a minstrel's button—"ta-dum dum"—that is winsome, and in the context of the song, heartbreaking.

> They hadn't been gone but a very short time
> Scarcely six weeks to the day [ta-dum dum]
> When death, cold death, spread through the land
> And swept them babes away.

My fascination with this song—its power to pull me off the highway—is probably inexplicable. Or, more precisely, it is an inexplicable mix of sounds, words, and silences that causes the ballad to be shot through with mystery and delights. The banjo's syncopation and strong backbeat make a bumpy ride for the overly solemn and offer up enough joy to fend off the beasts of loneliness, but the modal tuning, with empty spots for the sixth and seventh notes of the scale, keep the ballad focused and serve as a reminder that it, like life, is a pyrrhic victory over the forces of the night.

My fascination may have to do, as well, with the mix of pagan and Christian imagery that lodges the song deep in the culture. The children—the babes—do not come back from the grave wearing hats of woven birch as they do in the original Child ballad from ancient England, but they are studying the bewitching "grammarie" in that resonant place present in all folk geographies, the "north country." The meal in West's version is unmistakably a Christian ceremony, but it is, also, a "feast," as it is in the Child ballad, and the mother does make a bed for the children "in the back-most room," as she does in the pagan version. Above all, the title, "Usher's Well," which persists in most mountain versions, is steeped in associations with pagan "water" rituals. These vestiges of ancient religious practices cling to the newer Christian version. It is not a matter of new wine in old bottles, or an "emasculation" of the ancient text, as one writer put it, but a graft of the ancient to the very old producing now, and for as long as the song is heard, a deep and enriched sense of humanity. What knocked me off the road was the compound ghost of myself—of all my selves—riding into the now on a voice in my car cassette player but extending far back into the cold, silent nights of my Indo-European ancestors.

From the first measure of "Usher's Well," I felt the shock, the cassette player sounding above the ticking engine, but I registered another, more telling, blow later as I kept listening and the song, working its way through—not against—time, became a ballad.

"Only time will tell"—that is what we say. It is a hard lesson, setting the ballad apart from song. A song celebrates now—the moment—and laments its passing. The song longs to hold for all time that which is fleeting. Bettie Sellers turned to Reece's lyric "We Could Wish Them a Longer Stay" to explain the difference. Looking at flowering trees in spring bloom, Reece writes that they

Are lovelier, dearer now
Because they are soon to go,
Plum, peach, apple and pear
And the service blooms whiter than snow.

"Dearer because they are soon to go," Bettie says, repeating the stanza from memory. "The theme not so much of death," she adds, "but the swiftness of life and secrets of mortality. I feel that kind of thread runs through the lyric." The lyric—like its cousin, the song—is a Keatsian urn, redeeming time, a verbal snapshot for eternity.

In the ballad, though, time is spent. "Step by step by step," Bettie says pounding out the rhythm in her palm. The sun is higher in the sky and Bettie's living room, all a yellow glow when we started to talk, has whitened to the corners, giving a sharper edge to shadows. The ballad, she says, "is a progression of movements, in time, space—in attitude." It is headed for some "goal" and is "ultimately celebratory," but very much "a progression in time." Time is not redeemed but used up, and used up in service to a lesson that only time can tell.

I once wrote a song that turned willy-nilly into a ballad. I had written songs before and had created music for the lyrics of others, but never a ballad. My wife and I were in the living room, she reading while I plunked away at my banjo. The night *was* cold so we had a fire going. On the rug in front of me were the first three verses of a song written on a folded sheet of paper.

Follow me into the woods,
See the light dance gayly,
Catch a breeze in your ribbon wild,
And we'll find true love, Sally.

In other stanzas Sally's gown drops "on the rocky shoal," her "yellow hair" spreads across the grass, and the ribbon falls away, getting caught on a holly branch, the lovers laughing at their folly.

So far fine. A love song. But in the last stanza I heard something else—some sinister overtone in gown, hair, woods, and laughter, some hint of evil in the ribbon snared on a thorn. The love song, I discovered, as I rode obsessively from one rhyme to another, had hidden within it a murder. Suddenly the song took a turn—a gift of the night—and became a ballad.

> Wrap the ribbon round and round
> My love and do not dally,
> Muffle the baby's tiny cries
> And we'll find true love, Sally.

If I had stopped at stanza 3, I would have missed the ballad, but the fourth stanza allows events to have their way with love, telling a truth in time.

And what is the lesson that any ballad, in time, will tell? At the end of Reece's ballad, the horseman, mad with desire for his wandering wife, holds a knife that glints in the moonlight. "I've sought her through the earth," he says, the "magic-metalled knife" rising in fury above his head, "I'll seek her now beyond." The power of the night—the glittering moonlight—guides the blade.

In "The Unquiet Grave," one of the ancient Child ballads, a husband sits by the mound of dug earth for a year and a day mourning for his lost love. At last his wife speaks to him from the grave to remind him that what was can destroy what is.

> 'Tis down in yonder garden green,
> Love, where we used to walk
> The finest flower that e'er was seen
> Is withered to a stalk.

In a mountain version of this ballad, she warns him that his obsession with past love is fatal—a kiss from her "clay, corpsy" lips would bring death—but he cannot resist.

All that we love we lose—that is the lesson that time, in any ballad, will eventually tell. "Barbry Allen," as it is sung by Peggy Patrick, a friend of mine who was born and raised in the mountain town where I live, puts this truth simply.

It was in the merry month of May
When green buds they were swellin'
Sweet William, he, on his deathbed lay
For the love of Barbry Allen.

The "swellin'" of the green buds rhymes with Barbara's maiden name, but the "merry month of May" rhymes with "on his deathbed lay." Whatever makes us trip "lightly" down the stairs will one day knell in our hearts like a funeral bell, and that is true whether we act on the love or not. No matter what we do, loss will have its way with us. If we live and love, a "red, red rose" grows, ensnared, in "green briar."

No matter what we do—that is crucial. Ballads only *seem* to be morality tales about choice and responsibility. They always expose consequences, and in that sense are moral, but in the end they reenact the way that our moods, our emotions, and our obsessions possess us—*no matter what we do*. In ballads we have no control over our sorrow and happiness because, rose wrapped up in briar, the one bequeaths the other.

The ballad is a symbol of how little we have in the way of resources to bring to bear on our terrors. All we can do is keep singing. That is why ballads go on and on, almost endlessly in some cases. They do not time their revelations—*timing* is less important than *time* in ballads—so they are not fussy or artistic in that way. Rather they wear us down incrementally with all they reveal, just as life does. But the end does come, inevitably, inexorably, and driven by our bliss, we find a knife, glittering in moonlight, waiting for us there. Wrapped up in love that unfolds over time, our tears wet the winding sheet.

In "The Wife of Usher's Well" we hear the lesson about time and love and loss yet again. The children, who cannot eat the bread or drink the wine of this life that their mother has prepared, admonish her before joining Christ. They begin by forcing her—and us—to visualize the grave, that brown square of dirt where life's green comes to an abrupt end. Then in a sweet and understated way they say that her crying is futile because it wets the cerements of her lost children but not their liberated souls.

Cold clods of clay grow o'er our heads
Green grass grows at our feet
And thy sweet tears my mother dear
Will wet our winding sheet.

It is life's hardest lesson—and with children, what could be harder? It is the lesson born of night silences. It is the only answer to a mother's wail. When Bettie talks about the call of the mountain cat—the panther or mountain lion she heard one night behind her house on a hilltop—she describes it as the "womanlike cry of the painter." Nothing in nature is us, but it is just like us to give that screech a human voice, making a home of some kind for our babes. The night offers up its inhuman call. The ballads which say that love and loss share our lives are our oldest answer.

The Phrygian Mode

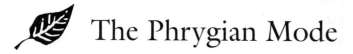

Like a woman hiding part of her face, music veiled in modes is mysterious, never revealing all of its secrets. During the Middle Ages scholars hunted throughout the modes for sonorous correspondences in order to uncover the secrets of the system. Like astronomers working in a Ptolemaic universe, they spun elaborate explanations in search of a simple key. Plagal variations, notes opened below the tonic to accommodate lower voices, nudged the tonic away from its position at the center of the musical universe and allowed a more comprehensive way of understanding music to emerge, one based on accidentals and major and minor scales. When plagal modes are sounded, the tonic is vulnerable and less certain. Buried in the middle of a string of notes, it can get lost, the ear tempted to hear, below the tonic, new possibilities for an ending. "Such fallen closures,*" writes Bronson, "are particularly characteristic*

of the Appalachian mountains." Ancients were suspicious of plagal tones, calling them inauthentic. In them they heard the death of the modes.

When I want to nudge myself off center, I walk up the road from our house to an old graveyard hidden in a patch of oak and pines. All the markers—hidden in lichen and moss—are crudely shaped. Like sails on the rolling sea, they lie strewn about, some toppled, others leaning as if they had ridden this rocky earth long enough.

No one knows who is buried here—there are no names on the gravestones—but I have heard intriguing rumors: runaway slaves, perhaps thieves. More likely it is a burial plot for a family of early settlers. When I stand among the stones on a drizzling morning, I am in the Phrygian mode. Here no birds sing and the three notes of the rain—mi, sol, la—*patter so lightly and quickly they make a single whispered sound. In the Phrygian mode, the groan of saws cutting winter wood reverberates in the valley every Saturday afternoon. The shaggy hide of mountain ridges shows through the bare, skeletal branches of winter trees, and the creek, so jolly in spring and a happy relief in summer, turns sinister, glittering like a knife in the sun and going gunmetal gray on cloudy days.*

"Pretty Polly, pretty Polly" the Phrygian tune begins. It is an old English broadside ballad about a man who murders his pregnant girlfriend, but as it traveled to America—shedding verses along the way—the motive for the murder was dropped or forgotten and the song became a dirge, a late winter cry about the inanity of life. "Come go along with me," Willie insists as he leads Polly into the woods, "before we get married some pleasure to see." She is reluctant and afraid, fearing that he will lead her "poor body astray."

There is, I think, as I walk home in the freezing drizzle, leaving the toppled gravestones behind, something of the plaintiveness of corrupted innocence in what Polly says. She knows him and knows she cannot stop him. He answers with the most chilling stanza in mountain music, a casual, brutal sentiment, the perfect foil to her naïveté. "Oh Polly, pretty Polly, you're guessin' about right," he says, a black hole opening in the dark earth of the song. "I dug on your grave the best part of last night."

Silence

Last week, when I had open-heart surgery, new photographs from the Hubble spacecraft showed stunning images of red-shifted stellar collisions moiling in absolute silence near the edge of the universe, and, for a time, the music in me stopped.

I'm forty-eight.

I first noticed the heart problem on nightly walks with my wife, Barbara. On the second lap around the small campus where I teach, she would begin to outstrip me, and I had to hold her arm to get her to slow down. One summer night I felt funny in the chest just above the heart, not a pain or soreness, just a pinch or, more accurately, a presence, an awareness that something I had never felt before was there.

When we stopped walking the feeling went away, and I dismissed it at first. I don't smoke, I eat well, and I exercise. My blood pressure is usually low, and my cholesterol is at the low end of high. I am generally healthy, and when my doctor retired several years ago I never bothered to get a new one. I guess this is what getting old feels like, I thought, when I took my wife's elbow to get her to slow down. I did not suspect heart disease.

There was another clue of danger. I sing in Butternut Creek and Friends, a local folk group that performs at benefits and festivals. One night during practice I noticed that I was short of breath at the ends of solo lines, and when I did harmony parts with my friends, I had to drop out before they did. This is ridiculous, I thought, as my friends merrily finished out the lines for me. My body, I think, was talking to me, and reluctantly I began to listen. At the ragged edge of breath and at the end of a nightly walk, in a place that was normally silent, there was a little scratching, a little emptiness. You're in trouble, it said.

In the fall I lined up a doctor, had a physical, did a treadmill test. My teaching job kicked in, as usual, but I was also in the midst of many projects by this time, most of them musical. The group is busy during early fall, and we performed several weekends in a row. I was also at work on essays about music in our area, which meant doing interviews and making music with local musicians at their homes during the week. I even entered a Georgia Mountain Fair banjo contest, which probably caused several lifetimes worth of stress.

Unfortunately, the treadmill test was positive, which meant that I suddenly had a cardiologist, too, who made an appointment for me to have an angiogram at Saint Joseph's Hospital in Atlanta. We set it for Thursday, October 30, so that I could do one more performance, this one with my son, Sam, at the Cherokee Coffeehouse, near the college where I teach. There was a steadily increasing sense of alarm—one thing leading to another—that would accelerate, but at this time I still thought that a simple operation like angioplasty was the likely outcome, plenty of time to squeeze in a few tunes.

Sam and I live in different musical worlds right now. He likes alternative rock-and-roll, and his musical hero is Kurt Cobain. My favorite music is old time mountain fiddle and banjo, and my favorite musicians probably live within fifty miles of my house. We change cassettes each time one of us gets out of the car. But the one area where our musical interests overlap is the guitar blues, songs in the tradition of Huddie Ledbetter. Early in the summer we began playing together on the porch doing old blues numbers like "In the Pines," "Midnight Special," or "The House of the Rising Sun." I sang and strummed chords while

Sam added the lead guitar. Together we worked up about ten songs, including a jazzy version of "Mary Had a Little Lamb" which just happened one night as we played. "The fleece," I sang, "oh, the fleece was white as snow."

We decided to try out our songs on the ears of friends at the coffeehouse and drew in maybe twenty listeners during the course of the hour. We knew these people and were not nervous. I plunked out a few banjo tunes, a friend sang a couple of folk songs, and then Sam and I got started. Sam thought that, in the tradition of singers like Muddy Waters, he should have a pseudonym. He chose "Coughing Tuna," so I introduced us with a few lame jokes about whether to call him Mr. Tuna.

"In the pines, in the pines where the sun never shines," I sang, "makes me shiver the whole night through." Of course I ran out of breath at the ends of lines, but no one noticed since Sam usually picked up those silences with a bit on his guitar. He also dug into the leads, playing well, attacking strings with authority, and I was very proud of him.

"I'm glad we got that in," I told Barbara without thinking much about it, but later, when I remembered the remark, I registered some of its morbid implications. "Got that in before *what?*" I asked myself, packing up the instruments so that they would be out of the way when I was gone.

The last task of writing I took on before going to the hospital in Atlanta was to revise a review of Sam Pickering's book *The Blue Caterpillar and Other Essays* that I had written for the *Georgia Review.* Stephen Corey, the associate editor, whom I have known for a long time, compounds the irritating habit of always being right in his critical comments with a tendency to offer alternatives that are precise and lyrical. Most of the time I hate him. All of his suggestions for the revision of this piece began with cutting—cut, cut, cut—which was, if nothing else, premonitory. He and Stan Lindberg, the editor at the *Review,* also thought that I was excessive in my praise of Pickering. "When we hit the 'greatness' paragraph on page four," the editors complained, "and when that is followed by the sentence linking Pickering with Homer, Joyce, and Proust, everybody is in trouble." I guess I did get carried away. It took an hour at the computer to tone it down, though I kept a few of the comparisons, offering a fuller rationale in each case. It had been a chore, but when I printed the copy and shut down the computer—the machine snapping and zipping to a halt—I took odd comfort, as I faced the possibility of my own end, in the fact that, for Stephen, a draft of any kind is reluctantly final.

By nine o'clock the next day I was in Atlanta, on a table in the cardiology unit of Saint Joseph's Hospital, prepped and ready for the test. At this point I still hoped that nothing else would be required. Though I've never thought twice about eating fried chicken, french fries, and pizza, my wife and I and the family generally ate well, home-cooked meals with lots of pasta and vegetables and fruits. Barbara and I also walked for about forty-five minutes three or four evenings a week and enjoyed it. I thought this trip to the hospital might be a fluke, and that I would leave with little more than a revised diet and a prescription for a new pair of walking shoes.

"Have you been here before?" the nurses asked at each of the check stations, as they prodded and poked and attached me to machines. When the last nurse asked the same question as he and his assistants lifted me on the operating table, I balked. I did not like its implications of recidivism and told him so. He laughed. "Most of the patients don't have to come back," he said.

An angiogram is a way of taking a picture of blood vessels in the chest. A small probe is inserted into an artery at the groin and snaked to the heart. There it emits a fluid that reveals, on a television monitor, the clogged arteries. According to the picture on the screen, one of my arteries was 99.9 percent blocked. I would need angioplasty immediately.

A boon and curse of angioplasty is that the patient is awake the whole time and watches the procedure on the monitor overhead, the same monitor that the cardiologist watches. I had met my cardiologist once before, in my hometown after he had read the results of my treadmill test. Now he stood above me, his face covered by a mask, as his hand worked the tube at my groin, and we both watched the image on the screen. The artery, widening at the blockage into a balloon of blood, looked like a dammed lake. I watched as the probe inched forward, through the ballooning section, and attempted to open the blockage on the other side. The image took up the entire bottom third of the TV screen. Each time the probe tried to enter the clogged section, the whole artery seemed to dance away. Other probes were tried, but the result was the same—the sludge in the artery was too hard to cut through. The pain in my chest slowly, but steadily, increased and I was calling out numbers—4, 6, 7—to indicate the level of pain, with 10 being the pain I imagined would occur with a heart attack. The doctor said little while he worked—mostly instructions to his assistants, especially when the lights in the room flickered—but at one point I heard him whisper, under his breath, words I won't forget: "I hate to see this in someone so young."

Bypass surgery would be required.

Everything happened quickly now. There was fear of a heart attack. A nurse leaned toward me and said the hospital had better than a 95 percent success rate with open-heart surgery. "You will need eight weeks to recover," she added. I met the surgeon, a smiling young man in a business suit who introduced himself. "You'll be fine," he told me. Then I met Barbara, who was fighting back tears. She held my hand, and we said a few words. Barbara is a worrier in good times, so I could imagine the torment she was going through and hated all this for her, but not for long. In a few minutes I was on the operating table and asleep. The last thing I remember was someone running his hand over the inner thigh of my right leg.

The universe consists of a violent mix of stars gathered into blobs, clusters, and whorls that collide and explode. The earthbound sense that the stars are isolated and permanently fixed against a dark blue backdrop is an illusion. "Gazing at the night sky, at the lights that seem eternally glued onto the black of space," writes Sharon Begley, the author of the *Newsweek* article on the latest photographs from space, "a star-watcher would never guess at the violence that lurks within the starry seas of tranquility."

The photos come to us from the Hubble Space Telescope, a wondrous eye on the universe located 370 miles above earth. When the telescope was first launched into space, there were problems—the eye on the heavens had an "astigmatism"—but in 1993 astronauts made improvements on the lens, and since then the telescope has been able to see deeper in space. Since light takes eons to travel such distances, it also sees farther back in time than anyone had dreamed possible, creating extraordinary photos.

The photograph of the exploding star Eta Carinae shows an ultraviolet center, where the explosion is brightest, surrounded by large reddish lobes filled with dust that absorbs the blue light. The Cat's-Eye Nebula, in the constellation Draco, shows the fossil of a dying star with a bright, white light at the core and a far-flung cloud of red dust about it. Most ominous of all, though, are the "Pillars of Creation," a stellar nursery in the Eagle Nebula. Star "eggs"—"*e*vaporating *g*aseous *g*lobules"—are hatched in clouds of gas that rise six trillion miles into space like robed figures, some capped in a nimbus of light and others rising to gargoyle-like masks, Halloween figures patrolling the universe in a ghoulish masquerade with stars exploding in their vast, dark gowns.

On Halloween I was moved out of intensive care and into my hospital room. It was a harrowing night. Early on there had been a party: staff, as well as patients who were well enough to play, gathered in the hall. Costumes, on the part of the patients, were optional, I suppose, since most of us looked sufficiently ghoulish without makeup. I was still too out of it to participate in the party. But when a nurse came to my room to take my blood pressure and temperature, I did try to join in the fun.

"My, your lips are pale," she said, the noise of the party muffled by the door closing behind her.

"It's my costume," I whispered.

Since I had not planned on this surgery, some basic information given to heart patients in advance had to be given to me under duress, and much of it, apparently, did not sink in. I did not know, for instance, how to sit up in bed. I couldn't just lean straight up the way I usually do, and I hadn't learned to lean against my elbow, a trick I picked up later. As a result I kept slumping further and further into the sheets.

"How you get all down in the bottom of your bed?" one nurse asked when she checked on me. "Pretty soon we won't be able to *find* you down there."

The biggest problem was my confusion about drugs. I did not know that the nurses depended on me to tell them when I needed painkillers. As a result I went through the night with only one pain pill. At times I was very sore, so I lay perfectly still, aware that the pain created an eerie sensation of emptiness in my chest. We normally don't feel the interior organs of our bodies, but now that four or five parts inside of me had announced themselves, I could feel them. They seemed to be hanging in the empty space of my chest cavity, jostling and colliding when I moved and lumbering to a bumpy, awkward state of tense suspension when I held still, my heart like a mobile of galaxies dangling in the void.

The first word I uttered when I woke up from the operation was "water." I have often heard that the dying want water and now I know why. I was hooked to tubes that gave me liquid, so I did not need water, but my mouth had never felt so dry. Of course, the nurses could not give me water. "The last thing you want to do, honey," one told me, her hand on her hip, "is throw up." Later, when I coughed for the first time, I knew what she meant.

My second word was my wife's name. She was there by the bedside and moved in quickly to take my hand and kneel beside me when I woke up. She told me that the operation had been a complete success. I had not had a heart attack, so there was no damage to my heart. I could expect complete recovery by January.

"Will I be able to do everything?" I asked.

"Yes."

"Will I be able to sing in Butternut Creek and Friends?"

I'm not sure why I asked that question. Just before anesthesia I vaguely remember telling myself that I would have to give something up, slow down, give my heart a break. This is not what the doctors would later tell me, but it was what I had thought going into surgery. I could not give up teaching or writing, so music would have to go. I guess it was still on my mind when I woke up.

"Yes, you'll be able to do anything, even sing," Barbara said, smiling now that I was awake.

Later, though she issued a warning to me. I would not, for a while, be able to play my new banjo. It was too heavy. She had weighed it, stepping on the scales without it and then with it. I would have loved to see her do this: hugging the banjo in the bathroom while standing on the scales—it was, I imagine, a sight. It weighed nearly ten pounds, and, since ten pounds was the absolute limit of what I could lift after surgery, she thought it too dangerous for me to lift and play.

"You can play your old banjo," she said. It was only five pounds.

Barbara's antipathy to the banjo is understandable. Let's face it, among my generation you expect to marry a guitarist—half of the baby boomers have a guitar in the closet, so the odds are good. But when a man takes up the banjo in midlife, a spouse is allowed to feel cheated. This is one of those fates, like falling in love with someone who develops a fetish for snake handling, tattoos, or rollerblading, that spouses have a right to think they have escaped. But Barbara assured me that her warning had nothing to do with her feelings about the instrument, and I believed her. She was afraid that I would hurt myself doing something I loved.

The warning was unnecessary. I did not want to play music at all, certainly not the banjo. Sam, my son, had carefully rigged up a portable CD player with headphones, and I tried to listen. He had selected some of the music he and I enjoy—Dylan's basement tapes and old Band stuff. Some blues by Scott Ainsley. I had some Fast Folk tapes with songs by emerging folk artists that Butternut Creek might use. Barbara had thrown in Schubert, our favorite composer—his trios for strings and piano.

Halloween night I tried to listen to the folk music but could not bear it. It sounded like noise, like people yelling at me and throwing stones. The CDs that Sam had sent affected me the same way. I took off the headphones, turned off the machine, and began the long slump into darkness, sliding inexorably in silence to the foot of my bed. Silence, apparently, was all the music I could bear.

The next night I did find music I could listen to—the trios of Schubert. To me Schubert has all the power of Beethoven but it is laced with a nearly lethal prettiness that Beethoven would rarely allow. The string trio in B-flat, played by the Grumiaux Trio, was beautiful from beginning to end, the violin, viola, and cello lines moving among each other as one sound with subtle, nearly imperceptible shifts of emphasis from one instrument to the other. The piano trios were at times hard going, a little percussive for my silence-hungry ears, but the "Nocturne" by the Beaux Arts Trio at the end of the CD was close to perfection, a lovely melody shared by each of the instruments, rising in power and force, the sound through the headphones filling me and drawing me to the last notes, a few light taps on the piano and a final string chord, to launch me into the silence that followed. If it hadn't hurt so much I would have cried.

Schubert's music is *gorgeous*—really there is no better word for this power and loveliness combined, so smooth and sweet on the ear that it is as close as music can come to the silence that engenders it. The CD got me through that night, and the next. After it finished, I lay in the quiet of my room until I fell asleep.

Some say there will be weeping and wailing and gnashing of teeth when we die. Others bargain for a heavenly chorus. My bet: silence. After surgery I was, I guess, getting used to it.

It is fitting, I suppose, that the cover of *Newsweek*—for the week that I had my operation—was given over to the most striking photograph from the Hubble Telescope, a picture of the colliding Antennae Galaxies, billions of stars crashing in a reddish swirl and shot through here and there with the white of new stars. "It looks like something under a slide," Barbara said.

The Antennae Galaxies are located in an area of space that scientists have identified as "The Deep Field," a spot of night sky so distant from us that the light we see from it has taken eleven billion years to reach earth. Looking at this image, we see not only far away but long ago, and what we see is a mighty cauldron: two star systems merging in a huge conflagration, stars crashing into each other or passing near enough that gravity tears them apart. A stellar mess. And yet, because there is no atmosphere, this enormous and ancient stellar ballet plays itself out in complete silence, just as the sun, buffered by empty space, explodes with thermonuclear abandon in absolute silence in the sky above us.

I saw the *Newsweek* my first day home from the hospital—it was on the kitchen table, I think—the Antennae Galaxies exploding noiselessly on the page. At first glance I thought of blood, the heart's stuff—a wound in the night sky—but when I looked again into the mute swirl of crashing stars, I thought of Schubert. I thought of the "Nocturne."

My operation was good news. With 99.9 percent blockage in one artery, I was probably close to a heart attack that might have killed me, especially in the remote area where we live. Since I did not have a heart attack there was no damage to my heart, so my recovery in January would be complete. Though he had gotten under my skin, the surgeon clearly did not know me, as his examples of complete recovery revealed. "You could skydive!" he said. "You can water ski!" Barbara laughed. In the surgery he had used the mammary artery, which lasts many years. My other heart arteries were only partially blocked and still functioning, so the veins from my leg provided backup, just in case. Clearly the surgeon did not want to go back in there for a long time. "You have a new heart," he said. "It's fixed. Eat well, exercise, and don't worry about it."

Still, I felt some nagging anxieties. Since there was nothing in my way of living to justify early heart disease, the cause was probably heredity, which led Barbara and me to worry for my children. My brother, when he heard the news, made an appointment for a stress test, which

I thought smart. Our older kids would have to be tested, too. I was also worried about myself. Forty-eight is pretty early to start this sort of medical problem. In the silence of that harrowing Halloween, when demons seemed palpable, the words of my cardiologist haunted me: "I hate to see this in someone so young." I had always thought that I would live to be an old man, playing banjo on the porch without a tooth in my head. Suddenly that possibility seemed remote.

One of the first calls I got when I came home was from my local hero, Ross Brown, an eighty-eight-year-old mountain fiddler with an international reputation who happens to live just down the road. Ross knows me as "that banjo player," even though I have played music with him on his porch seven or eight times. "I guess," Barbara says in his defense, "when you get that old you don't have to learn any new names." He called to wish me well and tell me that his son had recently had bypass surgery. "He had a time of it," Ross said, his son contracting pneumonia with a raging fever that gave the doctor fits. "He's doing just fine now," Ross told me, "and so will you."

I congratulated him for winning a prize, once again, at the Georgia Mountain Fiddlers Convention, and told him that I had a new banjo that I had to show him. He promised we would get together on his porch as soon as the weather got warm and I was well. "You take care of yourself, and I'll be seeing you," he said. The call lifted my spirits, but when I hung up I had the eerie sense of hanging up on my own future, which had, in a few days, grown vague and anonymous.

"Big Bang," the name of the reigning theory of the origins of the universe, is a misnomer. The universe, the theory argues, began in a cataclysmic instant of time, an explosion some fourteen billion years ago that created all of the matter and energy we know. The earlier view, the

"Steady State" theory, had argued that the universe was eternal and without a beginning, but in 1965 scientists detected radiation from the original fireball of creation, from the Big Bang itself. By now almost all scientists have shifted to the new view.

The theory may be right, but the name is wrong. There was no atmosphere to transmit sound in the first moment of creation. There may have been light, but even that is unlikely since photons, which transmit light, came later in the creative process. What is certain is that the big bang was less than a whimper. It was a soundless explosion.

Silence is the norm in the universe. Sound, voice, music, even noise—all that can be picked up by the human ear without the aid of electronics—is trapped in the envelope of our atmosphere. There may be other planets with atmosphere out there, no doubt there are, but they are equally isolated pockets of sound. The rest, to use an old phrase, is silence. When scientists replace Hubble in 2007 with the Next Generation Space Telescope, one that can see back fourteen billion years, perhaps to the Big Bang itself, there will be no bang at all.

Silence is our beginning—and our end.

Catnapping between urinations on the first night back from the hospital, I had a vivid dream. Barbara and I had come home over the mountain that day on winding roads, which no doubt prompted the vivid sleep images. In my dream I was facing out the back window of a car on a mountain road that went straight up. At first I saw mountain scenery along the steep road—trees, rocky outcroppings, occasional views of other mountains—but when the incline became completely vertical, all that was near quickly receded from view, and I had a panoramic view of treetops, roads, cars, farmland, and mountaintops. All the while I could hear the happy sounds of voices and car noises and the radio, but that soon gave way as we crashed above the clouds and the atmosphere at incredible speed and details of the landscape merged, revealing the larger forms of the earth, the mountains a mere ruckle in the surface with city lights tucked in here and there. Soon these lights flickered and faded, the earth becoming a dark surface, its bowed horizon visible at the top of my dream window. One by one the noises fell away too, first the car sounds, then the voices of loved ones, and at last the radio with a final squawk, and still I ascended, catapulted ahead and feeling afraid, but only mildly afraid, as all around me got dark and silent.

After talking to Ross, I tried to bang away at my old banjo, the one I was still able to lift into my lap. I had trouble holding my left hand at the top of the neck where I fingered chords and notes, and the stroke of my right hand over the strings was simply irritating. It sounded terrible. "Surgery not only improved your heart," Barbara said when I described how awful it was, "but your hearing too." No, no, I insisted. It sounded worse than usual. So I let the banjo sit, mute, much to the pleasure of the rest of my family. I put the "Nocturne" on the stereo.

There were signs even then that the old music was merely dormant in me. On the third day home I caught myself singing the old song "Sail Away, Ladies," about cheating death through the post office.

> If I die in Tennessee,
> Sail away, ladies, sail away,
> Send my bones back C.O.D.
> Sail away, ladies, sail away.

It is true that when I picked up the banjo occasionally, it still sounded bad, but I heard—as I usually do with this bedeviling instrument—the prospect of future improvement. Music would come back.

But I knew, in a way I did not understand before, that beyond the twang, beyond all the lovely commotion we make in a lifetime, huge amorphous forms rise in silence against a backdrop of emptiness. Silence is our fate. It is hard to come by on earth now. Even where I live, a neck of the woods far away from the city, cars can be heard in the distance, and the night is a cacophony of insect sounds. But the winter of my recovery is coming, and sometimes in the dead of winter the nights around here get very still and quiet. I'll always have music, I carry it in my head when it is not on my lips, but I think, from now on, I'll take time getting acquainted with its elder sister, silence. It is time to make a friend of her as well.

The Lydian Mode

They dot the hillsides—foundered, weathered, and gray—the ramshackle buildings of the earliest white settlers here. Unpainted sheds, barns, wells, and houses tilted toward the ground and moldering like an abandoned woodpile. Some old houses, draped in kudzu, are dragged to the ground wrapped in green youthful tendrils. Most collapse of their own weight, disintegrating in rain, sun, ice, and snow, sinking into the earth. A few stand on cleared land like weary boxers, shriveled by sun, battered by winds, awaiting the inevitable blow.

Occasionally we notice these, caught in a momentary glow of early morning sun or set off by darkened woods, called to our attention by their incongruity with the land. Most of the time we pass them without noticing. Broken and weathered, they have taken on the soft, smudged lines of their surroundings, like woodland animals curling up to die in hiding, wearing their end as camouflage.

The beauty of the dulcimer, Jean Ritchie writes, is in "the challenge of its limitations." The same, of course, could be said of life in the mountains. A life spending itself within a few predictable rhythms is both the curse and vanishing beauty of this place. All of this is true elsewhere, where limitations return us to essentials—in any place that has a winter, I suppose—but here the lessons have, if nothing else, their own music.

We come to our limits in the Lydian mode. Deep in the winter of its scale we hear mostly silence, an emptiness we can no longer fill. "Mostly silence" means mostly drone, since silence is the meeting ground of the mind and the barely audible. Lydian silence resets us, amplifying our thoughts, our breath, and all the ringing that lies deep in the inner ear, a music of regret at the threshold of sound.

"The lonesome days of winter they bring both frost and snow," one old Lydian tune begins. "Dark clouds around me gather and stormy winds do blow." In the song a man whose lover refuses to marry him decides to cross the "briny ocean and never married be," claiming "hence e'er" to choose a single life." In the Lydian mode a clinker falls onto the hearth, cutting a glowing trail, and we kick it back with a boot to where it dies in a bed of gray ashes.

There is no wind anymore—the storm is past—and the sky is blue, pristine, and filled with icy glitter, a borrowed light. We crunch through crusted snow, the dog shambling behind in a flurry and tumble, all paths obliterated by white, and make our way before the tall dark trunks to the creek flowing along the icy path it has made for itself. Who in the Lydian mode can resist poking a walking stick into the happy palace of frozen waters, the crystal walls crumbling in patches under the blows? There are no memories here—if that is what we came for—the creek is too much itself to serve as a mnemonic, and, anyway, it's too cold. We come here to feel the crushing weight of all that we have not done or cannot recall and gauge

our losses when all is gone. It is not sadness that brings the walking stick
crashing against the ice, and the dog, confused, scrambling up the bank,
but a calling out in weariness—the arm brought down by weight alone.
Sometimes, in the Lydian mode a drone is all we hear.

High Lonesome

"Get a window seat," a friend told me before I left for Portland. "The view of Mount Hood is worth the trip." So when I signed on in Atlanta I got seat 27A, right by the window, forgetting that the plane took off at 7:00 *at night*. A night flight. Four hours of solid black below me. The plane rose like a tenor note into a minor chord of darkness, all of America hooded in murk below.

This junket across the continent was my first long trip since undergoing heart surgery five months earlier, certainly my first flight, so I was a little apprehensive. The drive out of the mountains where I live had gone smoothly enough, the winding back roads of the hills releasing me in their own good time to the wide roads of the city. I got lost in Atlanta—where Georgia 400 runs into I-75—twice making a loop that hurtled me back in the direction of home, but I often get lost driving in cities and had allowed plenty of time, so I wasn't nervous. The long wait in the airport didn't bother me either. I was glad, temporarily, to shed my small-town identity and enjoyed anonymity.

But as the plane taxied down the runway I felt an unfamiliar pang, and when the wheels lifted off the tarmac, the anxiety increased, becoming an unmistakable hollowness, a melancholy that the ludicrous images of James Bond and exploding cars on the in-flight movie could not subdue. I was homesick. Like the mountain children I teach, I had a sudden and unshakable urge to go home. The stars—even the familiar band of lights in the belt of Orion, clearly visible through my cabin window—did not bring comfort. "High lonesome," I thought looking at the blinking red light on the starboard wing of the plane.

A few days before my trip to Portland I had heard the Powell boys perform at Chinquapins, the coffeehouse in Hayesville, North Carolina, just across the border from Georgia. The Powells are from Young Harris, not far from where I live, and their sons—who are in their teens—are already well-known musicians. There is nothing fancy about the appearance of the boys on stage, no sequins or fringe or sheen, just jeans and shirts and sneakers, but they play and sing with authority. "They've been doing it all their lives," their father tells me. "If the crowd is thirty or a thousand it doesn't matter. I don't think they've ever been nervous up there."

Wayde is a better banjo player and guitarist than anyone his age is entitled to be. His older brother, Nicky, who also plays guitar, is a tenor and sings in that high lonesome style of Roscoe Holcolm. When Nicky starts a song in the lower part of his range and you hear where he has to go to hit the high notes you think he will never make it, but he always does, the voice riding effortlessly up a ribbon of sound. It cuts through the chatter of customers, commanding the attention of everyone in the room at the same time that it sets him apart from the crowd. Wayde picks up harmony lines on the guitar, someone laughs, a waitress drops a plate—none of that matters. Nicky goes right on singing, undaunted, the center of attention and utterly alone.

I remember when Barbara and I first arrived in the mountains more than twenty years ago. I had applied for a job at Young Harris College, a very small mountain school. The drive into the Appalachians was lovely. It was spring, and the hills, hidden in low-lying clouds in the morning, changed to a deep blue by midafternoon. But we were from cities—New York, Baltimore, and Charlotte were our last three addresses—and not comfortable with the thought of rural life. When we drove into the town—at that time a motel, a country store, and a gas station—Barbara said "no way." You will be polite and *appear* interested, she told me before I went in for the interview, but there is no way we're moving here.

I don't know what Barbara felt, but I know what I was feeling. Cut off from the shopping malls of my suburban life, I saw misty mountains, Irene Berry's cows in town, and gray, unpainted houses here and there, and felt set apart and strange. High lonesome. Even with my wife beside me and our baby strapped into a carseat behind us, I felt eerily at odds with all I had ever been. This place does that to you.

That night we camped on a lake about ten miles from the college, and, after interviews and a campus tour were over, we walked the path through the campground, talking, weighing the possibilities for our future. Maybe we'll give it a year, we said. Nothing more. In the morning the lake was covered in wisps of fog, and across the way a dog barked. Mountains ranged around me, silent sentinels, the immense humps of earth shaded a misty blue making distance palpable by bringing the far away close at hand. I stood there under the scrutiny of their ancient disregard.

We decided to take the job and have lived here ever since.

Sometimes that first emotion of strangeness returns, a feeling created and sated by living here. I feel it now and then when I walk along Appleby Drive behind the campus and hear the voices of students on the ball fields below. Ten years ago we lived in the house on the corner there, and I liked to walk down my driveway to this spot to watch dusk fall on the fields and hear the shouts and hoots of young people echo in the hills. Now when I return I see once again the far-off batter swing, the sudden rush of bodies at play, and only later hear the crack of the bat, fresh, unmistakable, delayed, the echo taking a decade or so to reach my ears.

The resonant hillsides and shifting visual planes of the mountains create illusions that engender a sense of oddity and mystery. A walk up a mountain path lifts me high above the town I live in, miniaturizing all below and intensifying my emotions, an outcropping such as Sunset Rock becoming a perch on the world. A ribbon of smoke rides dusky currents of air into the sky *below* me, pooling and lingering there. On the evening walk back, the glowing light ahead is the lamp beside my wife, who lives this hour of my life far off but in view.

This high lonesome mix of love and loss is probably universal, but writers like me are particularly susceptible. The poet John Logan has written that a baby, weaned from its mother's breast, begins moving its mouth as if to shape words. Language begins with our first loss. For writers it never stops. They console themselves, redeem losses, with shapely words. Art does not begin in ego—Freud knew this—but in a sense of self-annihilation, the artist shaping a surrogate. The potter throws a pot. The painter catches a scene. The musician holds a note.

The writer fills his mouth with a word.

When as a boy I was told that my mother had killed herself, I hid under the stairs in the unfinished basement of our house and listened to the footsteps of a worried family above my head until someone came to get me. When I walk in the woods near my house at night I sometimes have the same feeling, the stars in scattered formations splashed across beams in the makeshift dome of the sky like a thousand nailheads. We are all orphaned in the world. The writer knows this, and the mountain writer, living in a landscape evocative of the maternal, perhaps knows it best of all. Our songs and words are a child's cry in the dark.

There is another kind of loneliness—call it low loneliness. I felt it when I woke up from heart surgery in intensive care. A crew of nurses hovered there attending every need, but in intensive care needs are great enough so that no amount of attention makes the aches and pains go away. Talking was hard. Movement out of the question. All of my attention was focused on the device I held in my right hand—a red call button. When I mashed it, women came.

The nurses talked to me as if I were a child. What choice was there? I could barely speak. I couldn't walk. I lay there. I mewed and groaned. I *was* a baby. I heard echoes of myself in other beds, other patients bitching and being irritable and trying to find some comfortable position, but it didn't stop me from bitching and being irritable myself, and no position sufficed. All that I needed was near—at hand—the distances collapsing in on me, and yet there was no nearness in anything at all. Numb from medication, I seemed to float, or, more precisely, my internal organs—normally unnoticed—floated and bumped with thick clunkings deep in my chest, dirigibles tethered by arteries and veins to the interior walls of my body, and I, adrift in an ether of painkillers, was likewise tethered to my bed by needles and tubes and weariness.

The voices of those I loved—who wandered, occasionally, in and out of my circumscribed semiconsciousness—sounded far off, and if I had not been so out of it I might have thought of those voices in the mountains that travel down a mile of a crooked valley and yet seem like a whisper in the ear. When I heard my name and opened my eyes, there was the face I love kissing my forehead, and the hand I love holding my hand, and the voice I love sounding miles and miles away. Low lonesome.

I rose high above all that by heading to Portland for a conference of writers, a gathering of several hundred lonely souls pretending to be otherwise. We sat in groups of twos and threes at breakfast, talking over rolls and coffee, and could have been a band of happy burghers here for a small business convention as far as anyone could tell by our bad jokes and easy laughter. On a car ride through town a street-corner evangelist proselytized us at a stoplight, but we kept our cool. We kept our little secret. Not one of us, as far as I know, stood in the middle of an intersection shouting, "I am an orphan to the world, emptying words into the abyss." No, we were on our best behavior.

At night, in the hotel room, I passed the time by playing the ukulele, learning the World War I tune "Pack Up Your Troubles." I got my uke, like most of my instruments, from my dad, who picked it up in Hawaii. It is a lovely Kamaka made of curly koa wood. The ukulele is fun and portable. In despair that I would have to leave both Barbara and the banjo home on my trip, I threw the uke in at the last minute.

Ukulele means "jumping flea," the instrument being small but mighty. By the time I get going on it—around 2 A.M. usually—banging out the melody in tiny chords up the slim neck, I can really make a racket. There is more high and happy in the ukulele than high lonesome. A "kit bag" for packing up sorrows when you are far from home, it is hard to play the thing and not "smile, smile, smile." I took it as a good sign when folks in the room above stomped on the floor. I assumed they were dancing.

In "The Prelude" William Wordsworth, the nineteenth-century Romantic poet and a mountain boy from the Lake District in northern England, describes a night when the shifting planes of his mountain landscape filled him with awe. He had stolen a rowboat—an "elphin pinnace," he calls it—and, dipping the oars in the water, made a silver track of "small circles glittering idly" behind him in moonlight. It was, he wrote, "an act of stealth" and "troubled pleasure."

Wordsworth, who eventually became the aloof and stuffy poet laureate of England, had been a scamp as a boy, robbing eggs out of eagles' nests and stealing from animal traps. Nature and the mountains were at this time "all in all" to him. In "Tintern Abbey" he writes,

> . . . the sounding cataract
> Haunted me like a passion; the tall rock,
> The mountain, and the deep and gloomy wood,
> Their colours and their forms, were then to me
> An appetite; a feeling and a love,
> That had no need of a remoter charm,
> By thought supplied, nor any interest
> Unborrowed from the eye.

So, with an eye trained on the horizon beyond the stern, the boy Wordsworth glided surreptitiously onto the lake at night, the moonlight cutting a path behind and nothing above but "the stars and the grey sky." Suddenly, while he watched, "a huge peak, black and huge," appeared above the horizon, "upreared its head," animated as if "with voluntary power instinct" blocking out stars and becoming a looming presence. The mountain was chasing him! Terrified, the boy quickly swung the boat around and returned to shore.

The mountain had not moved, of course. Hills beside the shoreline had obscured taller, more distant mountains, and, as Wordsworth rowed into the lake, his line of sight shifted, so he could see the far-off peaks—they appeared to rise precipitously on each stroke of the oar, gobbling up the stars. The illusion, pumped by physical exertion, guilt, and a lively imagination, filled the boy with dread:

. . . After I had seen
That spectacle, for many days, my brain
Worked with a dim and undetermined sense
Of unknown modes of being; o'er my thoughts
There hung a darkness, call it solitude
Or blank desertion.

No familiar sight remained untouched by the experience. Instead, ordinary events were cast against a backdrop of "huge and mighty forms" that "moved slowly through the mind" during the day and "were a trouble" to his dreams.

Wordsworth, the good old boy from Cockermouth, had discovered that high lonesome feeling. The mountain spectacle had cleared the way for a poetry of the sublime.

Sublime, yes, but lonely, an ache hard to bear and nearly impossible to leave behind. "I'm goin' down that road feelin' bad," one song sung in our mountains begins. The singer is going where the water tastes like wine, where the chilly winds don't blow, and to a happy kingdom identified as "the new regime"—a grand place no doubt—but despite the hope for his destination, he is still, in every chorus, feeling just plain bad. The farther we get from home the worse we feel. The mountains may have filled Wordsworth with fear as a boy, but in college "'mid the din" of Cambridge he often thought back on their "beauteous forms" in "hours of weariness" and felt "sensations sweet" that brought "tranquil restoration."

Push followed by pull—that is the tug of the mountains. Jean Ritchie wrote a song called "Last Old Train's A Leaving" that catches this double quality, the sense of awe that simultaneously attracts us to the mountains and drives us away. In the song we stand on a mountain while timber burns and folks leave, and are tempted to go ourselves, but, hearing night birds call "poor will," watching fields being plowed afresh, and seeing a redbud tree in blossom, we know that we cannot leave. When the "Last Old Train" pulls out we will not be on it.

The conference in Portland was great fun. Essays are not reporting but shaped works of art, I argued from the uncomfortably high perch of my panel on the first day. They don't tell the truth; they create it. After a verbal knock-down-drag-out with friends who hold to a simpler view of truth and a more demanding sense of obligation to the facts, I was declared a liar and let off the hook for the remainder of the weekend.

I attended a session on the achievement of the late William Stafford, the quiet poet from Portland, Oregon. Stafford believed that any fact was the end of a thread that could lead us back to the source of all things, the spirit. Our job is to respond. "Only the golden string knows where it is going," Stafford once said, "and the role for the writer or reader is one of following, not imposing." I sensed some contradiction between his ideas and my notion that artful language is shaped as well as received but took solace from his views anyway, knowing all too well my own desultory way with words. Certainly he would not mind that I snap a hem into the otherwise shapeless garment of my prose. Even after I take them in a bit, my essays hang pretty loose.

In downtown Portland I discovered Powell's, not the singing brothers from my hometown but one of the largest and best bookstores in the world, a survivor, still, of the chain-store massacre of privately owned shops across the country and the kind of place that a writer from the mountains of Georgia can get lost in for weeks. It is, in fact, a sort of mountain—a mountain of words with a map at the front entrance—and despite the map I did get lost.

Fortunately my new friends sent a party in after me and dragged me to a Greek restaurant—another treat not found in Georgia north of Athens. There we drank wine with a name made up mostly of vowels and had a merry time arguing about facts and truths and the little that words can do about them. "The criterion of greatness is not truth," I argued, a bit too loudly, drunk on diphthongs, "but whether the words make us feel less lonely in the world." I had, I see in retrospect, consumed more than my share of vowels.

By the last day of the conference, enough of us lonely souls had met that we were running in packs through downtown Portland and had to reserve a table for fourteen in a downtown restaurant—a huge goodbye meal. We talked about basketball and Portland weather and fathers and daughters, which gave us all something to say. One woman recounted the woes of her childhood, the rest of us falling silent before these facts of life, but soon the food came, and the waiter, delivering the best from Portland's microbreweries, asked us which states we were from, and in a happy geographical melee the gloom was dissipated. We left the place late that night with lots of hugs and laughter and happy talk of seeing one another next year in Albany, New York. It was lovely. It was happy. It was what remains when lonesomeness departs. And yet, that night, I went back to my room and plunked out a ukulele song about all my troubles and thought of home.

On the plane ride back from Portland I got to the airport early and claimed a window seat again. This time it was a day flight, and the skies were blue so we had a perfect view of Mount Hood out of the window. My friend was right: the sight of this mountain is a trip in itself. The snow-topped peak, a part of the Cascade Range and the highest spot in Oregon, rises more than eleven thousand feet above sea level.

In the distance it looked artificial and unlike any peak in my mountains, the tree line distinct, the hood of snow like frosting. A white-tipped breast. Springtime happens in the valleys around Mount Hood, but the peak is perpetually buried in a thick, snow-bound winter. As we flew closer, I studied the craggy slopes at the snow line, hunting out promontories and rockface, and as we flew directly over the mountain my eye went to the snow itself, thick, smooth sheets of white glowing in sunlight, cut off, separated from the brown and greens that surrounded it.

It looked remote, indifferent, aloof, and perfectly still, but as I let my eye follow the mountain's humped horizon, I saw, amid all the stillness of that place, that the icy surface was not pristine but constantly agitated, the wind throwing thin, barely visible, swirls of ice-glitter into the air. It was lovely, turbulent, and serene at once. There must be a name for snow cast up in a nimbus, a halo of light above a high, lone mountain peak. A name, I thought, craning my neck to get one last glimpse of Mount Hood—there must be one for this glow of snow—and I vowed to look it up when I got home.

Dulcet Melodies

The audience chattered, their voices rising and falling like the rattle of cicadas. Little girls sat in dresses in the front row swinging their legs, and old men used programs for fans to beat back the July heat. The theater in the Keith House of the John C. Campbell Folk School was packed, and people were gathering on the porch and the lawn as well, some sitting in folding chairs, a few on blankets, the rest standing with arms akimbo, sentinels guarding the ragged edge where music and night sounds meet. Bob Dalcimer walked center stage and tapped the microphone. Butternut Creek and Friends, the folk group I sing with, was about to go on.

I sat in a wicker chair in a room backstage, pretending to carry on a conversation with Rachel, the bass player. After my third trip to the bathroom, I seemed pretty relaxed, and I suppose I made sense, since she responded when I talked, but I have no idea what we actually said, because inside my head a single question was roaring, drowning out everything else. What the hell am I doing here? I'm an English teacher approaching fifty, and a frumpy one at that. I like to read and talk about books. Why—a robed voice in the back of my brain intoned—would you get out on that stage in front of all those people with a banjo strapped to you?

Then Bob announced us, "Butternut Creek and Friends," and we walked out into the lights. Rachel and Don took spots in the back with the conga drums and a stand-up bass, and Jennifer, Mindy, and I filed in through a minefield of instruments: guitars, autoharps, banjo, psaltery, ukulele, whistles, and a variety of unnamable noisemakers. Out of this pile of wood and metal we were supposed to make sweet song. As I strapped on my instrument, the house lights went down and I was staring off into a summer night, the audience receding into the hush their applause had cleared for us.

They had come for an evening of dulcet melodies.

Dulcet is from the Latin word for "sweet," and Butternut Creek and Friends is nothing if not dulcet. In our promotional brochure we describe ourselves as eclectic, singing folk, blues, and gospel. Anything but bluegrass, we sometimes say. When I introduced the song "Nelly Bly," which contains the phrase "dulcet melodies," I explained that in my house many adjectives have been used to describe my banjo playing, and *dulcet* is certainly not one of them. But the vocals in the group smooth out the edges, even of my banjo's jangle, and if I had to think of one word to describe this motley gang of folkies, *dulcet* would probably be it.

The concert was great fun. "Make up a night," we sang in one song. "Throw in some stars. Add a full moon while you're dreaming." The crowd sang along and clapped. At the end of the show, the audience gave us a standing ovation and asked for an encore, and I imagined each of them, as they left, humming some dulcet melody of their own into a night that—invented on the spot—had gotten a little cooler, yes, but also a little darker.

Sweet, after all, says most of what we know about sad.

This summer, Brenda and I have taken up playing music on her porch. She picks her guitar and sings. I plunk along on the banjo and sing too. A friend of Butternut Creek and Friends but not a member of the group, Brenda is a biologist who always has a project going on around her place. The back of her pickup is filled with empty milk jugs for hauling creek water to plants that cannot take the tap water from town, and in her side yard, not far from her porch, she has a compost which we hardly notice—unless the wind blows our way.

It has been a hard year for Brenda. Her father died and then her husband. Her mother has been ill, and she has been to the hospital several times herself for heart problems. Still, we sing. She was born and raised in the mountains of Tennessee, so she knows old songs like "Shady Grove" and "Mole in the Ground." "My dad used to sing that to me," she said, when we did "The Crawdad Song." Once her mother and nephew were visiting and joined in, and sometimes friends passing by walk over to listen or sing, too, but usually Brenda and I sing alone together.

Our favorite tune is the old gospel number "Farther Along." She takes the lead, and I come in with harmony for the chorus. The song, a blunt confrontation with bitterness, is about learning to live with others' good fortune in the face of your own bad luck:

When death has come and taken our loved ones,
Leaving our homes so lonely and drear,
Then do we wonder why others prosper,
Living as sinners year after year.

Bad luck, the song says, makes us feel like outcasts, lost souls who must "labor and weep," cut off from the happiness of those around them.

The song carries us deep into woe, letting us share the sadness with another voice, so that, for a while, the burden falls away of its own accord, and we can live with what we do not understand and cannot bear. Once we make the song our own, the words are always there, at our lips in times of trouble. A song solves nothing, of course, but with it we can, as another tune that Brenda and I sing puts it, "pack up our sorrows" and move on.

"Farther along we'll know all about it."

Song is part of the mission of the Campbell Folk School, where Butternut Creek and Friends performed. "I sing behind the plow"—that is the school's motto, and people come from around the world to this spot in Brasstown, North Carolina, to hear mountain music and learn mountain crafts. Envisioned by John C. Campbell and founded by his wife, Olive Dame, in his name in 1925, it is a place where students learn by doing. To study math, the first students built a barn. To learn history, they asked, "Who is your momma? Who is your daddy?"

My favorite story has to do with Olive Campbell herself, who taught geography by giving lessons in cooking. As the women worked in the kitchen preparing food for students, she would keep a globe nearby and teach them about each of the places that the spices they were using had come from, finding the far away embedded in what is near. Now people come here to learn pottery, chair caning, blacksmithing, enameling, woodcarving, storytelling, and much more by doing these activities with a master craftsman in a beautiful mountain setting. "I sing behind the plow." Maybe the motto is as good an explanation as any of why I was standing on the Keith House stage.

Between songs I told the audience that I loved the phrase and couldn't resist blurting it out, often at inappropriate times, an activity that got me into some trouble at home. "One afternoon," I told them,

> while I was sitting on the porch with the banjo on my knee, my daughter walked by carrying her puppy. "I sing behind the plow!" I announced to her, smiling. "I *wondered* what that was," she said to her puppy, without

missing a beat, nodding toward my banjo. "I knew it wasn't a musical instrument."

Later, as my son walked by, I tried again: "I sing behind the plow!" I should have known better. Eating a cupcake and drinking a tall glass of milk, the smart aleck came armed with a look of adolescent disdain. "That's fine with me, Dad," he said, before taking a big bite of chocolate, "as long as you're plowing the *lower* forty."

"Undeterred," I told the concert audience,

I waited until my wife walked by wearing her gardening hat and carrying a spade. She looked innocent and daisy-fresh in that getup, giving me a false sense of security. I wanted to grab her and roll down the hill into the tall grasses, but suspecting that such shenanigans wouldn't do, I tried the motto on her. "I sing behind the plow!" I intoned, my banjo still squarely in my lap. "Terrific," she said. "But I wish you'd try singing behind the lawn mower."

Sometimes, I know, singing is not enough. Consider Butternut Creek —the stream that lends its name to our musical group. It is one of many troubled waterways in the mountains, where development has not been accompanied with concern for protecting the land. The river begins in springs in the gap behind the Presbyterian church not far from my house and flows just beyond the town of Blairsville into the Nottely River. Since I have lived here we have had a blizzard, a hurricane, and—most recently—a tornado, which have altered the appearance and even the course of the river, but it is the activities of those of us who have moved into the area that have done the real damage. Silt from construction has made the water cloudy, even at our house, which is near the source. Farther along, in Blairsville, it picks up so much septic and industrial runoff that it stinks most of the time.

Damaged and fragile as it is, the creek still inspires the group that is named after it. We practice at my house once a week, the band members crossing a wooden bridge over the stream to get to my place. Occasionally we sit on my porch, the babbling ripples in earshot joining in, I guess, as the evening gets dark around us. Many of our favorite songs—"Muddy Waters" and "River" to name two—are about rivers, and one song, written for us by a friend, is called "Butternut Creek."

But songs don't save rivers. "Black waters flow into this land," Jean Ritchie wrote a generation ago about the destruction of pristine mountain areas by modern industrial life, and the destruction continued. More than a year ago, I wrote a song about the ecological damage in our area. Called "Wind in the Appalachians," it uses language from old-time religion to censure environmental destruction. We must, the song says, repent and change our ways environmentally as well as spiritually. Since the song was written the creek has gotten worse.

Often I *do* wonder why we bother with songs. Singing—as we all know—inevitably brings humiliation in its wake. A sour note, broken string, or forgotten lyric waits farther along in every musician's future. Disappointment is just down the road as well. Believe me, Butternut Creek and Friends does not always sing in places as fine as the folk school. Ross Brown, the old fiddler from Hiawassee, got his start by playing at hog killings, and while Butternut Creek and Friends never played at a place that wild, we have had our share of unusual gigs. Once we performed in a parking lot that was so hot the autoharp picks kept slipping through Jennifer's fingers and my tapping toe stuck to the tarmac. I also remember singing at a church social that was so packed no one could hear our amplified voices above the noise of the crowd. The line for food passed right in front of us, and people would stop to say hello and carry on conversations with us *while we sang*. One man asked Mindy for a date.

"I'm trying to sing here," she said at last.

"I don't care," he snapped while our guitars gently wept, "I'm trying to talk to you."

Most of the time at parties or festivals we are background, and people don't listen at all. We played at a garden club party once, and I saw a good friend in the crowd checking out all the plants. She passed right in front of the stage, looking intently at the shrubs placed in front of our feet. When I asked her about it the next day she said, "Oh, you were there?"

But even when we are making fools of ourselves we keep singing, usually in three-part harmony. Voices in unison have the dull grandeur of a Gregorian chant, but harmony creates a rich sound by setting the voices against each other. At practice, Mindy, who can hear harmony lines in her head, patiently gives us various vocal parts until we get a mix we like, and Jennifer listens hard, alert to those times when the parts overlap or slip into octaves. Beauty is in the mix: different voices brought together on different notes making one sound. It is a joyous paradox.

Most good harmonies stagger the voices, and occasionally two of us will hold a note while the third will move, one voice finding—really creating—a new chord out of the steadfastness of the others. It is a lovely moment in any song as two voices gather at the changing of a third, making something new. I think of friendships, fragile and ever-shifting. I think of our lives, so many crisscrossed lines. I think of the currents of a river, some eddying, others flowing, making one mighty whole.

Wisdom is found in opposition—the ancients knew this. Socrates believed that knowledge proceeds by dialog, a friendly debate, and is best taught in conversation. But harmony, too, is a kind of dialog. Setting opposing voices free from the tyranny of speech, harmony delivers words to all the sounds they can muster. The words themselves may be the same, but the vocal lines soar to different levels, combining and picking up fresh nuances along the way. Sweet opposition—it is a great teacher.

Opposition also sets the songs themselves in motion. "I loves all you pretty women," one verse of a famous blues song by Huddie Ledbetter begins, the next line reinforcing the sentiment with a twist. "Yes, I loves you all the same." But the last line of the stanza delivers the truth, in opposition: "Don't loves you enough to change your name." When Jennifer sings "Once I lived the life of a millionaire," from another familiar blues song, we know, from the first word, where this tune will take us.

Bitter comes with the sweet. It is the truth of all music, though gospel songs have a different way of delivering the message. In them the joyous truth of this hard life is delayed, reserved for the next world. A dulcet change is coming, yes, but it is found down the road, down by the riverside, over yonder.

The sad are one note away from happiness.

And the happy are one note away from woe.

For the song "River" Mindy plays the mountain dulcimer, a simple, three-stringed instrument with a lovely, double-bouted hourglass shape and a haunting sound. Most players hold the dulcimer in their laps, fingering the strings with one hand and strumming with a quill or a thin pick in the other. It is the most feminine—even maternal—of the mountain instruments. Jean Ritchie, who first popularized the dulcimer and often came to the Campbell Folk School to sing and play, says that many mountain girls were forbidden to play the fiddle, so they took up the dulcimer instead. In pictures of her, the dulcimer looks like a baby in her lap.

I run my fingers over a dulcimer that I made several years ago. Set in the Lydian mode—a scale with a wintry feel—the instrument gives off a mournful sound, the tuning limited to sad notes. There is grandeur here, I think, as following an impulse I move to the second note of a melody that I've not decided on. In this mode, I am free to choose any note on the diatonic fretboard, but no matter where my finger lands the song will be sad.

The last few years have brought sadness and hardship to each of us in Butternut Creek and Friends. One of the original members of the group quit after a heart attack, preferring to devote his free time to physical exercise. Another got a divorce. Others have had more literal storms—hurricanes and tornadoes—rip through property, changing the landscape by tearing down hundreds of trees. Last October I had bypass surgery.

Rachel Caviness—our bass player—tells the story of her move from Atlanta to the mountains. She and her husband, Connie, had bought mountain property in Hightower, beyond Hiawassee, and had planned to move there when they retired. "We saw the waterfalls and these beautiful woods," she told me. "It was just what we wanted." In 1989, a week before they were to begin building, Connie died. "He would have loved it as much as I do," Rachel said. "It was a shame."

I would say that we get through hardships like these one song at a time, but that's glib and not exactly true. Something deeper and more important than just "getting through" happens when Butternut Creek meets week after week in my basement. Sorrow, as Langston Hughes once wrote, "mellows to a golden note." Songs do not remove—or even ameliorate—woe. Woe is built into them. Our melodies may be dulcet, but they are mixed up with the inevitable sense of the end that is inherent in all beauty. The songs may endure—with parts set years ago and ringing in countless reiterations—but the sense of time passing and life changing is made palpable as voices, accustomed to new joys and griefs, rise to the old notes yet again.

Our most requested song is "River," a tune that Butternut Creek and Friends has been singing for many years. When the instruments stop at the end of our version, Mindy, Jennifer, and I keep singing the last measures a capella and in harmony to a room full of silent listeners. The song is so familiar to us that when we performed it this time for the folk school audience I just floated along effortlessly, without much thought, until we got to the a capella ending. Suddenly, I felt an emotional jolt—a *frisson* of recognition—and knew in that instant why I stood before this audience with a banjo strapped to my body: we lay our burdens down when we kneel at the bank of a song.

Butternut Creek and Friends sang "River," here on this stage, many years ago, the first time we performed at the Keith House. Before we became who we are now, we held out these very notes in this very place. The trees in our backyards stood taller, then, rivers and arteries flowed clear, and hearts were intact. Much has changed since. We are a little farther along, and I know, in a way I did not fully understand then, that there are only so many songs left in us. But then and now, our patched-up and temporary lives gather at the river of a dulcet tune, where none of those changes matter. For the length of an a capella chorus, we hold our silent instruments close to our bodies, sing our hearts out, and meet at forever.

The Locrian Mode

Maybe the Locrian should be called the "Sisyphus mode"—
you may find yourself playing in circles.

—Force and d'Ossché, *In Search of the Wild Dulcimer*

In the Locrian mode we leave silence behind: the silence of lovers gone and love not tried, of songs that we no longer know, though we hear them in our minds. The silence of a child running to us across a memory. The silence of a held breath, a caught breath, a last breath. In the Locrian mode we are past letting go.

The Locrian mode is an abstraction, a place that in theory must be on the modestar. In practice it is nowhere—and everywhere. The Locrian scale lacks a true tonic, so a tune in this mode is endless. The melody line, unable to resolve itself or come home, can't stop. It moves in the mind like a mobile, spinning forever on the same string. It is a Möbius strip of sound. It is the sound at the outer edges of the universe where stars, those scattered remnants of an explosion, move in consort, dancing to the music of the spheres.

Locrian is singsong. Not the Ionic ditty that accompanies jump rope or hide-and-seek, but that inane, childlike, and haunting up-and-down of a child's voice when the child is alone, talking to dolls or stacking blocks, a little murmur you don't notice till you put down your book or finish the dishes. Singsong. *The word itself says it all: tautological, alliterative, but out of tune at the vowels. "Merrily we roll a . . . , merrily we roll a . . . , merrily we roll a . . ."—but we never reach "long." Saccharine and crazy, like tangy sorghum syrup, you recognize it as the song of our childhood loneliness, too, and are aware that you have been humming it to yourself all of your life. The Locrian mode has been waiting all this time for you to come to your senses.*

Despite its foreboding, the Locrian is a springtime mode, because the place where all songs never end is also where they begin. The Locrian mode is unstable, its twinned heart the musical equivalent of the oxymoron: old and young, sweet and sour, breath and death; death and breath, sour and sweet, and young and old. It is what we hear when we sleep at night and at night what we sleep when we cannot hear.

There are no songs in the Locrian mode. It is where all songs end, or, more precisely, where all songs never end. I might say that the Locrian mode is chaos, just randomness and jangle, but that is not right, because there is pattern here. We are going somewhere, but we never arrive and seem—how did that happen?—to have forgotten where or if we began. In this game of musical chairs, a chair is missing but the music never stops; at this square dance lovers do-si-do and swing their partners endlessly, always looking unsuccessfully about the bobbing heads of this inane melody line for a familiar face and not finding one. Locrian music is the irritating tune of the merry-go-round or, as one dulcimer player put it, "a merry-go-round out of whack."

In the Locrian mode we fill silence with eternity and absent ourselves. The dulcimer may be tuned to the scale, but our mind and soul are elsewhere. We have at last got the ear of God, and it listens for us. Death, the Locrian mode tells us, is what we expected and stranger.

In the Locrian mode we are beyond being alone. We float among stars and planets floating forever away from stars and planets floating forever away. We have nothing to look forward to and nothing to lose, until a low moan, indistinguishable at first from the singsong sounds, calls us—at once and at last—and the stars and planets, too, call us back, away from the brink of never again. Clone *and* tone *and* monotone, *the low sound says, releasing us in time from timelessness into the past participles of our future doings,* flown *and* shone, sewn *and* mown—o, o, o—*the words moaning in the teeth of their consonants*—groan *and* crone, *and* bone, stone, drone.

The Big Scioty

To get to the Old Growth Forest Trail we ride Georgia Highway 180, a steep and twisting road that winds behind Vogel Park and cuts through Slaughter Gap, taking us deep into the Blood Mountain Wilderness. We head past Sosebee's Cove in the Coosa Bald Scenic Area, a wildflower paradise located in a deep ravine, and pass Lake Winfield Scott, a chilly gem on this brisk midwinter afternoon, staying on the highway until it dead ends at a high farm with grazing cattle. From there we follow a series of increasingly narrower roads—Highway 60, Cooper's Creek, Grady-Grizzle, and, where the road turns to dirt, park along the margin, ready to walk.

It is one of the last days in 1997. The younger children, Alice and Sam, are with me, Alice wearing a new pair of binoculars around her neck, Sam dressed in a flannel shirt and jeans. Matt, my oldest son, is there too, down from graduate school in Baltimore for the holidays. Getting out of the car and putting on jackets, we look up the gravel road heading over a hill into the gray trunks of a Georgia hardwood forest. We've packed a lunch and are ready to make a day of this trip—a journey into the Valley of the Giants, the only spot in our region that still has old growth trees.

December is one of the best times to walk in the southern mountain woods. Usually there is no snow, and it is still warm enough to get by with a light jacket or flannel shirt. Leaves are down, so that the ridges of mountains, obscured in summer by a curtain of green, can be seen undulating into the distance, a rumpled blanket of deepening shades of blue visible behind gray and austere verticals of hardwood trunks.

Most trails in the mountains get narrower as they go, road giving way to gravel, gravel giving way to path, and the path becoming little more than a laurel-fringed rut running along ridgelines and mountaintops. Somehow we had left the directions to the site in the car, so we chose our way by memory, and followed a trail that descended into the woods toward Mark Helton Creek. The winter woods were quiet, no sound but our feet rustling through leaves and the rush of the creek below. We followed the creek for a half mile and came to a log bridge, one that we had to cross on our hands and knees.

"I think that would have been written up in the directions," one of us said—probably Matt, who has suffered through these outings with me before. I'm always getting lost, whether on foot or in the car. When I'm in a good mood, I call it my natural bent for discovery. Usually I grind my teeth. We forged ahead nonetheless, the creek bed turning increasingly narrow, the rumble of the creek itself growing louder in the deepening chasm. Our journey was getting spooky, the way a trip down the wrong mountain path can.

A song began to roll through my thoughts, punchy like the rhythm of our footsteps, droning like the sound of the river that has been digging a groove into this hillside for eons. It was "The Big Scioty," a tune named for a winding river in the West Virginia–Ohio mountains. I had heard it from David Brose, a folklorist from Brasstown, North Carolina, who plays a sweet and eerie banjo. "The Big Scioty," he had explained one afternoon before picking it for me, "is a real twisty, narrow, dark river that's low. You have rock walls on both sides. Craggy.

Steep. Heavily glaciated." As I followed my kids down the narrowing path, the creek churning below us, the song wound through my thoughts like a litany: narrow, twisty, dark, low.

At last Matt, who was heading up our little expedition, stopped and turned to speak to us. He was all in blue: blue T-shirt, blue pullover sweater, and blue jeans. We came to a halt. "I think we're lost," he said at last.

By now the river was a torrent of sound, a drone that went on and on, with or without our footsteps, accompanying travelers along the ancient path to nowhere in particular. We went a little farther. For a while the stream got nervous, shallow and pebbly. Alice scanned the tree line with her binoculars, looking for the big ones. Sam ran on up the trail and reported that there were no big trees ahead.

"I don't think we could have missed them," I said.

Reluctantly we headed back up the trail looking carefully to the left and right to see if we had somehow overlooked a tree the size of a lighthouse.

Everyone knows that a banjo has punch. "It's a rhythm instrument," David says, tapping the banjo head with his index finger. "This is calf's skin. It's a drum." What we can forget as we walk the zigzag of a banjo tune is that it cuts a path through a steady drone. "There is a reason why a banjo has a drone string," David says. "It ought drone." Set against the percussive quality of the instrument is a continuous sound, a groan, a wheeze. "You can use the fifth string, as a drone," David says, "but you can also play off of bass notes, get the sustain of those low bass notes rolling." The drone can rumble like boxcars on a track, or ring sibilant, like rain. It is the comforting hum in the inner ear. It is wind above and creek below, I told myself as we followed the trail back to our starting point. Rhythm and drone—they lead the way. The heart follows.

Eventually the kids and I got back on track. We walked up the trail and down the gravel road to the car and ate lunch while we read through the directions again. We had missed a fork just before the log bridge, a narrower path less traveled. This trail followed the other side of the creek, but higher, winding along a thin ridge line. So we set out again, and as we walked this way I could barely hear Mark Helton Creek, though looking down the deep ravine it was possible, here and there, to make out the glitter of running water below, the baseline of our adventure.

This time we came across enormous fallen trunks on the crest of the ridge. Old chestnut trees, we thought, taken by the blight. They lay in moldering hulks. Several of them had fallen across the path, and we had to crawl over or under to get by. As the path wound out of the darkness of the creek, Sam ran on ahead, and Matt pointed to big tulip poplars here and there, the first sign of old growth trees.

"Wow," we heard as Sam came upon a giant poplar on the side of the path. "Look!"

Most of the old growth trees in the Appalachian Mountains were cut down in the great timber boom between 1880 and 1920. According to Ronald D. Eller, in *Miners, Millhands, and Mountaineers,* it happened in two stages. During the first stage agents from New England logging companies, which had already stripped the northern hills of timber, paid Appalachian farmers "on the stump" for select trees, which were felled and sent downriver to temporary timber mills. Select trees of hickory, yellow poplar, and ash—with diameters of four feet at the stump—went for about two dollars apiece. These logs were "snaked" through the mountains on wagons or sent downriver with spring rains. In some areas, mountaineers created "splash dams," gated dams upriver. When the logs were in place, the gates of the dam were opened, filling the river with water and propelling the enormous logs downstream, usually causing great damage to trees and shoreline along the way. "They'd let that water open," American Jarrell, a mountaineer from Brandytown, West Virginia, said in an oral history of Appalachia, and "it just look like a big thunder cloud a-comin'."

In the last decade of the nineteenth century the lumber barons got serious, replacing the temporary mill sites with permanent operations such as the one in Helen, Georgia, along the old Logan Trail or the Ritter Mill in Hayesville, North Carolina, near where I live. They built by railroad lines in places like Waynesville, North Carolina, or along rivers like the Big Sandy River in eastern Kentucky, where the Yellow Poplar Lumber Company set up operations. The work of these mills was so efficient that they stripped the mountains of trees by the 1920s, leaving a ravaged moonscape behind.

The boom began, ironically, when Asheville, North Carolina, a small city of two thousand, became known as a health resort in 1880 and grew to a city of ten thousand in ten years. It and the nearby towns of Tyron, Hendersonville, and Brevard were magnets for the wealthy who visited the region, including lumber barons who saw the possibility for timber here. One of these was George Washington Vanderbilt, who acquired 120,000 acres of land and built a French renaissance castle named Biltmore. It contains European paintings, fine tapestries, elegant antiques including rare porcelains in a mansion that rivals European castles, but on the entire estate there are no old growth trees. He cut them down along with the all the hardwoods in the Pisgah Forest surrounding the estate. By the turn of the century, the virgin timber on his land was gone.

Is anyone free of blame? When we built our house eleven years ago I walked the land with Dale Cochran, a friend of mine who knows about all things green. We marked off beautiful trees for protection: dogwoods, service, beech. We tagged grand oaks and a sassafras and set aside a pair of big poplars. Our builders were environmentalists who did their best to save all the trees we marked, but by the time we had cleared for a foundation and a workable site, put in a gravel drive and set sewer lines, most of the trees we marked had to go. The two grand oaks were saved by the careful work of the crew, but were too close to the house and died a year after we moved in; the stumps remain in the midst of flower gardens. Only the beeches—with winter leaves of gold—and the two grand poplars are left standing, the rest knocked down, buried or snaked off along Highway 76, the modern equivalent of a splash dam river.

Joyce Kilmer Forest in North Carolina is the last large tract of old growth trees. Other than that there are only pockets here and there, like this stand at the end of the Old Growth Forest Trail. As Sam shouted his greetings to one of the big old poplars, the rest of us stood in awe on a crest at the edge of the Valley of the Giants, a stretch of topped-out trees, each more than fifteen feet in diameter at the trunk, lonely sentinels to what we have done.

The binoculars that Alice was wearing around her neck had been a Christmas present. She loves musicals and goes once or twice each year to the "Fabulous Fox Theater" in Atlanta for shows, so we had decided to get her binoculars to help her see the costumes and faces of actors from the balcony. For some reason I was put in charge of picking out the gift, and stood for most of an hour in the optical section of Service Merchandise, where the binoculars were wired to a display case, scanning the room with each of the tethered possibilities. I felt deliciously clandestine and surreptitious, even intimate, with everything blocked out in my vision except a lit circle that carried my sight over great distances, though I also felt a little foolish each time I set down a pair, and the world, at arm's length and fully illuminated, came rushing back.

A good pair of binoculars, I surmised, comparing the price tags with my experience, does more than bring objects closer. It gathers light. As I synchronized the two unfocused tubes of the best opera glasses in the store on the handbag of some unsuspecting customer, the single bright disk that emerged glowed like a heavenly object in the night sky of my cupped hands. I thought of Dante's vision of God in *The Divine Comedy* as three circles of light superimposed, one upon the other into a single heavenly orb, three beings in one with a human face glowing from the center. We may not be able to name God—any more than we can tell the content of a lady's mind by the bag she carries—but if we are to bring what is impossibly far away close at hand we can, these glasses tell me, draw a clear circle of darkness around the little we can know.

Narrows define. In a leaf-fringed path we can see, on both sides, the edges we dare not cross, and learn to live in the grooves of our own making. We snake a way along the path, uncomfortable with limits, but dependent on them, too, each tree a lesson in the majesty of staying in our place. A tree is, in fact, a sylvan binoculars of sorts. A poplar digs in and sets its sights on the sun, its trunk rising over many of our lifetimes along a straight and narrow path of glorious illumination into the heavens.

It is the narrowness of this cove that protected these old growth trees, I realized, as the kids and I made our way deeper into the stand of giants. Enclosure kept them safe.

"God," David said holding the banjo in his lap, "some of that West Virginia music where I grew up—those tunings and those tunes—are dark: modal, eerie, dank. You just smell the coal dust and feel the humidity in the air—just spooky." When he reset the strings of the Tu-ba-phone to the Sandy Belle River tuning and ran an index finger over them, I got an inkling of the gloom hidden in the banjo's drum. The sound was cold and misty, like mountain fog. Impenetrable. A sound to get lost in. It *was* spooky.

Tunes follow a path, sometimes bright and sunny, sometimes dark and narrow. When David lights into "The Big Scioty," the path is shadowy and twisted, the sound haunting, staccato and howling at once. The fingers of his right hand come down hard and sure on every note, and the thumb cocks the high-pitched fifth string, pulling outward as his hand comes up, the way someone might pop open a can of beer, releasing the string each time with a ringing "ping."

With his index finger he hits the low drone, getting bass strings to resonate constantly in the background. Against this steady groan I hear a slide on low strings. It's a surprise, like water running uphill, going against the current of sound. "Oh no!" it announces. "Oh no!" it says again. "Oh no!" High above all this are the treble notes, a pretty mountain melody which sheds its prettiness against this backdrop and turns into a nightmare, an obsession, a Möbius strip of notes that fall back on themselves and start over. "It's a very crooked tune," David said before he started, "irregular," but as he runs through it for the third repetition, its pattern, at first elusive, takes hold deep. It is a tune to bring you down. Down into the grove. Deep into the shadows. Down into the narrows.

"And the song," David added when he was done, running his hands across the open strings again, "the song is winding and sort of reminds me of, I sort of hear that, that easy flowing right there, sort of twisted and"—and despairing of words, he took the banjo and played again letting the high notes glitter like jewelry cast away on the deep-running, feverish, doomsday undertow of the drone.

We walked dazed for a while in the Valley of the Giants. All of the trees are topped, storms having ripped out the crowns, but trunks still rise majestically above the leafy foliage of newer trees. One of the old growth lunkers—the largest tree in the Chattahoochee National Forest—has a trunk more than eighteen feet around. It is hard to imagine how old these trees are. I sing a song about a bristlecone pine in California that dates back to biblical times. These trees are not that old, but a friend of mine who is a biologist tells me that they go back more than four hundred years. As old as Shakespeare.

We took some pictures and posed in pairs in front of a few giants. I got one shot of all the kids by one. Then we took pictures of me with each of the kids in succession. It was great fun. I got the kids to circle a trunk, their arms outstretched, to show how wide it was. The three of them were able to reach about two-thirds of the way around it, and I got a picture of that. Then Sam started clowning, putting his arms around a sapling and straining as if he couldn't reach—so I snapped that shot too. For the last shot I took a picture of the kids with the Valley of the Giants behind them. Sam is in the middle—his mouth open—telling a joke as usual. Matt and Alice are holding back laughter. The trees rise behind them, a maze, it seems, of infinite and undifferentiated verticals. Around Alice's neck are the binoculars, twin tunnels of light made for a long, narrow, richly articulated, dense, but glowing vision of the world. We are all smiles.

Several months later I took an evening walk in the woods by our house and thought, once again, of the hike with the kids along the Old Growth Forest Trail. I walked past the service tree in full bloom in our yard, spring's harbinger, a narrow band of white rising in all the gray of the woods. I passed under the twin poplars that rise some eighty feet in front of our house. Less than three feet in circumference, they are far smaller than the old growth trees. "They have a long way to go," I thought.

I ducked into the woods, the path hidden by a dogwood branch, and followed the old logging trail along the creek, past the laurel where I play banjo, and on to the creek bend. There are wide, flat rocks there and viney branches of an old oak, and by steadying myself with the tree limbs overhead and stepping carefully, I was able to cross. From there I made my way through a trackless woods of saplings to Thomas Circle, an old mountain road.

At one time Thomas Circle was part of an Indian trail and later the main road between my town and places east. Now it is a paved semicircular spur hidden from the highway by a rocky hill. The oaks along Thomas Circle are tall and arch over the road like the buttressed ribs of a cathedral interior, a nave of green and shadows, with only a strip of sky visible overhead.

For several weeks I had heard wood ducks back this way crossing just at sundown, so I had my eyes on the sky in the hope of catching a glimpse of them. The ducks, easily seen on distant horizons in flatland, cross the mountain sky quickly and are hard to spot, but if I were ready I might get a look at them. I saw Jupiter and Venus vying for a corner of the darkening sky and, a little further up the path, the moon rolling into view like an unexpected guest. No ducks.

This is the way most of us who live in the mountains, hemmed in by high horizons and dense trees, see the world. Vacationers and outsiders build on the mountaintops and ridges. Most of the people who have been here a long time live in the valleys and coves, and rarely take in a mountaintop view. Ours is the high narrow view where a band of light overhead is made visible and sharp. Surprise is the gift of such views, a surprise as old as the trees in the Valley of the Giants. If we have binoculars, we look up.

Hello, moon, I thought, as I walked down Thomas Circle, the glowing lunar circumference so sharply delineated against the shadowy trees, a shiny dime in the darkening sky. That's when I heard them—the wood ducks, I mean—honking just beyond the tree line, and suddenly saw the quick pair dashing across the narrow band of light overhead, a drake with the hen-duck just behind, dipping and skittering. They flew through the moon, flashing a silhouette, and then, just as I turned, dashed past the glowing planets. Pumping and squawking, they disappeared behind a crown of trees.

The Drone

Drone, stone, *and* bone, crone, *and* groan—o, o, o—*the words moan in the teeth of their consonants*—mown *and* sewn, flown *and* shown—*the past participles of our doings, the drone submerging "now" in "before," our former joy in woe. With a slight broadening of the vowel we hear* wan *and* song *and* soon, *but these stray too far from the* oh *at the word's core, and it is the core, the low moan, that calls us back to* clone *and* loan *and* tone *and* monotone *and—the saddest drone of all*—alone.

"Drones are an accompaniment to life," Sheila Chandras says in discussing her CD called A Bone, Crone, Drone, *so I follow the birdsong—cardinal, I hear, and song sparrow—down the hill to the logging road, past laurel and rhododendron, the name itself a haunting drone, the birdsong accompanied now by the sound of Butternut Creek, and come on a rocky shoal where two streams merge. They are monotonously beautiful, the sounds at this meeting of creeks, the serrated edges of birdcalls endlessly*

repeated, the eternal clatter of water on stone in the creek bed, the quiet rush of all that falls through branches in the woods. Drones are always, it seems, about falling. Even the birdsong, happily varied between intervals ends on a dying note, telling the same tale over and over, all that happy ending in sad, all that dulcet drifting to morose as the sorcery of time and mood dictates.

In the West the drone is more insistent—a holy monotony laid bare along miles and miles of straight highway, identical fence posts, and a limitless, unchanging horizon. Here, in the Appalachian hills, along gently winding paths, it is gentler, a hiss, a whisper, a low lapping sound like a creek, its iterations more varied, but reiterated nonetheless, not the harmonica's low wail, but a sound more suited for echoing hills, a dulcimer's jangle.

Two of the three strings on the mountain dulcimer are set as drones that duplicate, or harmonize with, the ground note—the tonic of the opening chord. As the player strums the melody string with a feather—one traditional method—the quill brushes past the drones, sounding them, too. "This provides the melody string with a constant harmonizing chord," writes Jean Ritchie. It "gives the delightful and characteristic drone or bagpipe sound."

There is something tentative and unsure about tunes on the dulcimer, each new note of melody dragging with it the starting place, a past on its back, a voice from home crying out for the melody line's inevitable return to the tonic. The songs are usually composed of five notes, none of which strays farther than the range of untrained voices from the first. There is a potent and happy sense of completeness when the dulcimer tune returns to the home that the drone never let us forget. Like those languages where hello and goodbye are the same, the drone is a wave made of sound, hail and valedictory.

Drones are everywhere. "They're around in the form of streams," Sheila

Chandras says, "in the form of blood singing in our ears." There is the drone of a day of rain. Today it has fallen all morning like the end of something, a monotone it seems, but that is not true. Drones are continuous, not monotonous. If I listen to rain I hear many different notes being sounded: the babble on car hood, the staccato on asphalt, the thump-thump in flowerbeds. Rain whispers in grass and clatters down gullies or in drainpipes, the drone ever-changing and constant, like life, like the seasons.

"It's really coming down," someone says, standing at a window cradling a cup of coffee, the drone of some day dropping all about her. The drone is always about falling. Falling and rising and falling again—the undulant rhythm at the source of our lives. Hum a note deep in your throat and listen. Hold it. Repeat it. It is the end. It is the beginning.

The drone can be heard in the fifth string of the banjo, the plink, plink, plink at the withers of any mountain tune that instrument might care to ride, but the banjo does not have the most characteristic drone nor does its ringing match the sound hidden in the word drone, *the sound that the* o *in the word suggests. The drone is often low and nearly inaudible, barely there but ever-present, more like a pulse than some glitter at the edge of things, like a heartbeat, like breathing. It is, in European music, the ur-sound of the hurdy-gurdy and the funereal call of the bagpipe, and in India it is the whisper of the sitar. It is the bourdon of the open string on the fiddle, the resonant thump of the tabor, and the note hummed deep in the throat of the flautist.*

The drone is generative. It may seem to be holding the melody back, insisting it not wander, but such a harnessing of sound accompanies the spur of creativity, the drone a ground note, or a combination of ground notes, that suggest, even dictate, other sounds, giving an otherwise random string of notes a context, a history, and an identity which are the conditions of melody.

It is to song what sleep is to our dreams.

November Fields

It rained on the afternoon that the fiddler Ross Brown told me about the song "November Fields." Ross lives on a nice spot that overlooks the lake in Hiawassee and, beyond that, Harris Mountain. As I pulled up to his carport, the rain was still spattering here and there, but the storm was over, the clouds retreating across the water, hauling thunder and lightning on their dark shoulders. "I moved here in 1960," Ross said, nodding toward the houses across the lake, "and there was nothing but thirty acres of pine and oaks growing over there."

We gathered in the living room because of the rain. Ross, who is eighty-eight, looked tired, but he cracked jokes and smiled impishly. He wore a blue plaid shirt and pressed slacks—I have never played with him when his clothes were not freshly pressed and a little formal. As usual he had on a ball cap, this one saying "Hiawassee Oprey" above the bill.

Ross has taken his fiddle—and his mountain music—around the world. His favorite concert was at the Wolftrap in Virginia, but he has also played at the Smithsonian and has traveled as far as Seattle in the United States. He has been to Norway and Scotland and played two years ago at the Olympics in Atlanta. Ross has been playing the fiddle since he was twelve, originally taking it up, he said, to drive away his sisters. "I just did it to aggravate 'em."

In the early years he fiddled professionally, often with friends, Lawrence Eller and Lester Waldroup, playing everything from dances to hog killings. He refuses to practice, insisting that he should have the hang of it by now. "The first fiddle strings were them old catgut," he told us, "they'd squall on you like a wildcat." During the depression fiddlers wore out their bows so quickly they had to fashion a backup out of a willow twig, he explained. They'd "rosin up that stick real good and they could fiddle up a storm." He *has* been at it a while.

As he gets his fiddle out of the case he tells us about a scheme he has for selling apple brandy. Ross grows and sells apples and he had—he told us—too many this year. He figures that he and a friend could go in together, build a still, and sell the juice for forty dollars a bottle. "They used to make it up there on Hog Creek," Ross said. It provided a good excuse for making music. "There'd be a hundred and fifty songs to the gallon."

Ross's fiddle playing is lively, but there is nothing frantic or giddy about it. He takes tunes slowly, even the fast ones, his songs animated from within by a youthful and loving spirit. "It's a sweetness," my friend Rachel Caviness, who introduced me to Ross last year, says, and she is right. I have played banjo and guitar across from Ross's fiddle often this summer, and each time I have taken away new lessons about the sweetness of mountain music. But today as Ross played and talked, I heard something else, and got some sense of the cost of sweetness.

We played "Billy in the Low Ground," "Lost John," "Mississippi Sawyer," and "Fisher's Hornpipe." When we got to "Soldier's Joy," I remembered the first time that I plunked out the clawhammer part of that song with Ross on the carport earlier in the summer. "All the banjo players are going to the three-finger style," Ross said when we finished that day, pointing his bow at my hand. "That old time banjo picking is right now a lost art."

Loss was on Ross's mind this afternoon. He talked about the death of his friend Lester Waldroup. "I tell you, old Lester Waldroup was the only musician I ever heard of that actually played at his own funeral."

Lester had died of a heart attack a number of years before while loading up instruments after a dance at Clayton. "When they had his funeral," Ross said, "that's all they played was his religious hymns."

He talked about Winslow King, the well-known fiddle maker from my hometown. Ross is left-handed, and Winslow reworked a right-handed fiddle so that Ross could play it with ease. When a lefty plays a right-handed fiddle the strings are upside down, which is, Ross says with his usual understatement, "inconvenient." But when you change the strings, Ross explained, "it throws any fiddle out of balance." So Winslow made a special fiddle for him, moving the bass bar and sound posts and graduating the top. When Winslow died Ross played the fiddle at the funeral of the man who made it sing for him.

The hardest blow this year was his son's brush with death. His son contracted pneumonia after surgery on his heart and fell into a coma. "They got a quart of fluid out of his lungs and he run such a high fever that they had him packed in ice," Ross told us. "There was ten days he didn't even know he was in this world." Fortunately, the fever broke and Ross's son regained consciousness, but the ordeal was frightening. "He come a little of leavin' here," Ross said.

We played "November Fields," a song Ross says he wrote in the mid-eighties, some twelve years ago. It is a slow number, one of those songs that sounds a little like soft crying, and Ross—as he always does—played it clean, with feeling but without sentimentality, making each note "sing," as Rachel says. When we finished Ross set his fiddle on the couch beside him, put both hands between his knees, and told the story about "November Fields."

"I never did come across a fiddler who didn't say, 'I sure do want you to teach me that tune.'" Ross explained that his partner, Lester, created lyrics and sent off for the copyright, which he kept in the glove compartment of his car. Lester "nearly got in a fight" with one man over the rights to the tune, Ross explained—Lester planned "to make a million on it."

Lester was a card—a big man who "could grab a handful of weiners and just eat 'em right down." He was also, Ross said, the slowest man on earth. The group had gone to Asheville, to a studio named Hear! Hear!, to record. When they started, the sensitive equipment picked up scratching noises—the sound of picks that had, over the years, dropped into Lester's old Gibson. "What the hell is that?" the technician asked. It took twenty minutes for Lester to shake them out, and the delay irked Ross—"I never got so aggravated at a man in all my life." Lester also insisted on dubbing in each instrument separately—a time-consuming process. Eventually they cut six tunes, but the session was getting late—"way up into the night," was the way Ross put it—when Lester decided to add a Jew's harp over tunes that were already recorded. "Hell, I'm going home," Ross announced, "I'll not fool with it anymore." The group decided to quit for the day and come back on the next Wednesday to do the last six cuts.

But they never came back. That weekend they played in Clayton, and Lester "fell dead with a heart attack." Ross tried to get the others together to complete the recording so that Lester's version of the song could be released. "Oh yes, yes, we'll go," the others in the group said, but it did not happen. "We never did get it finished," Ross said.

Sometimes when Ross ends a story a hush falls over the group while we wait to see if he has more to say or if he wants to play music. So we waited in silence looking out the window. The storm clouds were gone, but the scene was still sunless, the lake metallic gray, and Harris Mountain was shrouded in mist. "November fields, you know," Ross added at last, picking up his fiddle again, "when the harvest is over in November and all the fields are put to sleep."